Small Websites, Great Results

Doug Addison

PARAGLYPH™
P R E S S

Small Websites, Great Results

Paraglyph Press, Inc.
4015 N. 78th Street, #115
Scottsdale, Arizona 85251
Phone: 602-749-8787
www.paraglyphpress.com

Paraglyph Press ISBN: 1-932111-90-5

President
Keith Weiskamp

Editor-at-Large
Jeff Duntemann

Vice President, Sales, Marketing, and Distribution
Steve Sayre

Vice President, International Sales and Marketing
Cynthia Caldwell

Production Manager
Kim Eoff

Development Editor
Ben Sawyer

Cover Designer
Kris Sotelo

Printed in the United States of America
10 9 8 7 6 5 4 3 2 1

3 3187 00222 9959

The Paraglyph Mission

This book you've purchased is a collaborative creation involving the work of many hands, from authors to editors to designers and to technical reviewers. At Paraglyph Press, we like to think that everything we create, develop, and publish is the result of one form creating another. And as this cycle continues on, we believe that your suggestions, ideas, feedback, and comments on how you've used our books is an important part of the process for us and our authors.

We've created Paraglyph Press with the sole mission of producing and publishing books that make a difference. The last thing we all need is yet another tech book on the same tired, old topic. So we ask our authors and all of the many creative hands who touch our publications to do a little extra, dig a little deeper, think a little harder, and create a better book. The founders of Paraglyph are dedicated to finding the best authors, developing the best books, and helping you find the solutions you need.

As you use this book, please take a moment to drop us a line at feedback@paraglyphpress.com and let us know how we are doing—and how we can keep producing and publishing the kinds of books that you can't live without.

Sincerely,

Keith Weiskamp & Jeff Duntemann
Paraglyph Press Founders
4015 N. 78th Street, #115
Scottsdale, Arizona 85251
email: **feedback@paraglyphpress.com**
Web: **www.paraglyphpress.com**

Recently Published by Paraglyph Press:

Degunking Your Email, Spam, and Viruses
By Jeff Duntemann

Perl Core Language Little Black Book
By Steven Holzner

Degunking Windows
By Joli Ballew
and Jeff Duntemann

Degunking Your Mac
By Joli Ballew

3D Game-Based Filmmaking: The Art of Machinima
By Paul Marino

**Windows XP Professional: The Ultimate User's Guide,
Second Edition**
By Joli Ballew

Jeff Duntemann's Wi-Fi Guide
By Jeff Duntemann

Visual Basic .NET Core Language Little Black Book
By Steven Holzner

The SQL Server 2000 Book
By Anthony Sequeira
And Brian Alderman

The Mac OS X.2 Power User's Book
By Gene Steinberg and Pieter Paulson

Mac OS X v.2 Jaguar Little Black Book
By Gene Steinberg

The Mac OS X.2 Jaguar Book
By Mark R. Bell

Monster Gaming
By Ben Sawyer

Game Coding Complete
By Mike McShaffry

Mac OS X 10.3 Panther Little Black Book
By Gene Steinberg

For those who taught me.

❧

About The Author

Doug Addison is a freelance web producer, journalist, and consultant. His company, Doug Addison Web Productions, specializes in website design, development, and maintenance for businesses large and small and includes among its clients McDonald Observatory, Aid to Artisans, Inc., and Motorola. As a journalist, Doug has covered the business, science, and technology fields for more than ten years. He also serves as a judge for the annual WebAward Competition. Doug lives in Austin, Texas, with his wife and two daughters. Visit Doug online at **www.daddison.com**.

Acknowledgments

Thanks to my family and friends for their support—and my clients for their patience—as I toiled away to make this book a reality. Thanks to Alison Macor, Stuart Wade, and Kenan Pollack for their encouragement and advice, and thanks to Paul Mitchell for his insightful comments along the way. Thanks to Tom Myer, who introduced me to Neil Salkind, who introduced me to Keith Weiskamp, my inimitable editor, without whom the book you hold in your hands would not exist. And thanks to the small businesses around Austin who provided me with good coffee, free Internet access, and—most importantly—a cool escape from my poorly air-conditioned office while I wrote during the hot summer months in Texas: Spider House, Teo, Austin Java Co., and Flightpath Coffeehouse.

CONTENTS AT A GLANCE

CONTENTS

INTRODUCTION

Size Matters, But Not in the Way You Might Expect

I'd like to start with an email. I want to send it to you, but go ahead and let anyone who is involved in the design and development of your website read it:

Dear Business Owner,

When was the last time you used a website that really worked? When was the last time you saw a website that wasn't bloated with more graphics, more pages, more text, and more possible ways to navigate it than the site really needed?

As a web designer, I know that more functional and better-working sites can be created if me and my peers put our minds to it and resisted the temptation to simply "design and build big." By taking the smart approach and emphasizing quality over quantity, websites can be more fun, more organized, more inviting, and much more successful.

I also know there are many reasons why most sites are designed and built the way that they are. Taken together, these reasons create a powerful obstacle to changing our ways and embracing a more focused, effective, and results-oriented approach to web design that really succeeds.

Don't worry. My commitment is to help both you and your web designer understand the benefits of designing and building a website that has the right scale. We'll get you back on track so your website can become one of the most powerful, useful, and well-liked parts of your business.

Sincerely,

Doug Addison

In this book, I'm going to discuss how we got to where we are on the Web today, and what's wrong. I'll then provide you with a blueprint for designing, building, updating, and promoting a site that emphasizes quality over quantity. I'll examine why today's often overly complex design and technology approaches have created a real mess. Let's face it; too many sites are cumbersome and artificially bloated. My goal is to convince you that there is a better way to create effective websites.

As you work through this book, don't worry if you don't immediately agree with, or even see the common sense of, everything I present. I'll make my case and give you some powerful, specific (and reasonable) strategies and tactics to take advantage of the Small Site approach. But I don't want you to just take my *word* for the importance of creating small focused sites to help your business succeed. I want you to see it with your own eyes. That's why I've filled the pages of this book with real-world examples of sites that follow the Small Sites philosophy. As you look over the dozens of screenshots in the course of reading this book, notice the pattern that emerges: the sites that do one thing right tend to do many things right. By the time you finish, I promise that you'll have an exciting new perspective, and see possibilities for getting results from your site that you never even imagined before.

Building Small, Building Wisely

If you're still not convinced, look at it this way: Today, people are craving smaller, high-quality experiences—in their homes, in their lifestyles, and in their hometowns. But by opting for smaller and simpler, they are not compromising on quality. When you design and build right with your website, it will provide users with the kind of experience that makes them want to visit and return. They'll also want to get to know your business better, which should be the real goal of your site.

Remember that in the early '90s most people thought the Web was only for techies and academics. By the late '90s, many people in business were worried that the dot-coms were going to make "bricks-and-mortar" businesses obsolete. Of course, neither point of view was correct. While millions of people stared at the dust (and the billions of dollars lost in market capitalization from the dot-bomb phenomenon), a much more select group of people quietly discovered the real business power of the Web. They have made money, kept customers, and in general improved their businesses using the Internet.

Their secret? They've learned to create websites that produce great results. But not everybody's happy with what's happening on the Internet today.

Here's the hard question I believe you should ask about your site: Who's being served? Take an inventory. Start with your prospects and your existing customers. Here are some of the questions you should be asking:

- Does your current site serve your business as a whole? If the best answer you can come up with is, "It tells people who we are, what we do, where we're located, and how to get in touch with us," this is a good start. But there is more that you can do as you'll learn in the pages ahead.

- Is your website easy to use? Do you often get complaints from users of your site that they can't find critical information? Would your customers rather use your 800 number to call and ask questions rather than use your website?

- What does your website say to your customers? What does it do for them? What does it make easier for them?

- How can you simplify your site? What pages can you get rid of? How much clutter do your customers have to wade through to get to the really important stuff?

- Does it make sense to have different, smaller, more focused websites for different purposes?

- Does you site support your sales and marketing efforts? How, specifically?

- Does your site meet the customer service standards you've set for the rest of your business?

- Does your site serve your bottom line?

If, at this point, you feel your businesses may be hampered by website bloat, you're probably wondering "What's the alternative?" Welcome to the Small Site approach. Starting with Chapter 1, I'll take a high-altitude glance at the reasons a Small Site might be the right choice for your business. Then we'll dig in and present the in's and out's of how you can convert to, and profit from, a Small Site.

Dawn of a New Era for the Web

We are on the brink of a new wave of activity on the Web—not a boom that will make a few people a ton of money, but a boomlet that will improve the bottom line for thousands of small business that heed the advice presented in this book. Google and Yahoo are striving to provide searchers with ever more targeted and local results. More and more people are going to the web before they go to the phone book to find a plumber, a realtor, a clown for their kid's birthday, or a place to take their in-laws out to dinner.

Businesses that are already online with a bloated and unmanageable site should use this book to refocus their websites for their customers who are doing most or all their business over the Internet. Small businesses who shunned setting up a website because they feared it would not be worth the time and money invested in it now have a playbook for themselves—and their web designers—for getting online in a small *and* successful way.

BUILDING SMALL: A NEW APPROACH FOR SUCCESSFUL WEBSITES

- Learn about the Small Site philosophy.

- Learn why big sites can be a waste of money and resources.

- Learn why large and bloated sites fail and why building small offers a better alternative.

How is your website working out for you? Is it a thriving and well-behaved ambassador for your business in the online world. Or is it out-of-date and overrun with unnecessary add-ons? Do you have difficulty keeping your site fresh and up-to-date because of its size and complexity? Or are you having difficulty even getting a website set up in the first place because you think you need to build a big site that includes all of the bells and whistles you encounter on other sites and you don't have the knowledge and resources to do so? If your business is like many trying to take advantage of the Internet these days, your website may have become unfocused, cumbersome to use and maintain, and expensive to manage—in a word, bloated.

In this chapter I'll quickly discuss some of the problems of building large, bloated sites and then I'll dive right into the Small Sites philosophy. You'll learn why building a small site is a smart idea in many cases, and you'll learn why more and more websites are following the principles of the small sites design approach.

The Problem of Building Big

A common mistake among small businesses that try to set up websites for the first time is the belief that in order to deliver a useful and popular site, they must have a big site that includes everything but the kitchen sink. But just as a physical store with too much floor space can be a drag on a business's profitably, so too can an oversized website be a drag on the potential of your enterprise's online efforts. This book is here to say, "It's okay to think small when it comes to your website."

Big sites are not necessarily bloated, and bloated sites are not necessarily big. Like all-in-one kitchen utensils, bloated sites try to do everything (it slices! it dices! it makes julienne fries!) and end up doing nothing well because the business that runs the site can't keep up or loses interest when the "new website honeymoon" ends.

Bloated sites are hard to understand and poorly organized—in a word, overwhelming. They tend to be built for the owner's or designer's benefit, not for the benefit of visitors and potential customers. They often emphasize over designed widgets and unnecessary features that drag down their usefulness and drive up their cost to run. Bloated sites often are out of sync with a business's other marketing efforts. Instead of absorbing some of a business's marketing efforts with the do-it-yourself, on-demand communication techniques at which the Web excels, they end up creating new work for a business. Visitors who can't find what they're looking for on a bloated site end up calling or sending an email looking for answers. In the end, bloated sites confuse visitors and turn away potential customers.

If you already have a website, it may have languished since the day your web designer cashed his last check. If you're still in the planning stages—still thinking about creating a "Web presence" for the first time—you may envision a flashy and easy-to-maintain site with e-commerce capabilities that lands at the top of Google's search results the day it's launched. No doubt, the pervasiveness of the Web these days has put pressure on your business (and your competitors)—no matter how small—to create a website or do more with the one you already have.

The key to success for many websites is to avoid the temptation of building too big. In fact, big websites that try to do too much often fail because they provide a poor customer experience. And in the end, the experiences that your customer comes away with from using your site is the most important factor. Just think about the last time you used a website to try to find out some information about a company's products or services. If you had to wade through pages of information just to find what you were looking for—such as the company's phone number—you were likely experiencing a real case of website bloat. Here are some of the more common signs of the bloat that large sites suffer from:

- **Slowly loading home page.** A site's home page loads slowly because it includes large graphics files, time-consuming videos, or sound and music. Personally, I just want to quickly run from a site that starts to play music or Flash-generated overviews.

- **Inscrutable or inappropriate graphics.** This goes hand-in-hand with the first sign. The last thing I want to see on a website is another group of "regular folks" looking up and out at me from my computer screen with that Lilliputian pose that tries to make me feel 14 feet tall. Or head-scratching clip art like the example in Figure 1.1. Or a stock-art image of a headset-adorned customer-service representative. Companies monitor phone calls for "quality

Figure 1.1
Maybe the owner's daughter created these offbeat illustrations for a
financial services company website. That's the only reason I can come
up with for why they're on almost every page on the site.

assurance purposes." Why wouldn't you be just as diligent with the
quality of your website?

- **Cumbersome navigation**. Websites that provide too many navigation options or complex menus and hidden links are often good
  examples of sites that need to be simplified. It's very easy to fall
  into the trap of creating a good website that provides useful content and features only to have the site fail because the navigation
  is so poor. See the example in Figure 1.2. If customers can't readily
  find important information on a site, they will think that the information was omitted. Their impression will be that the site is "so big
  and has a lot of information I don't really need, but they left out
  the really important stuff."

- **Emphasis on the amount of content instead of its accuracy or
  relevance**. When you think of the cost of printing and publishing,
  it's easy to see why people get the perception that putting up content on a website is free or doesn't require much in the way of
  resources. Many companies go wild in this respect and try to put
  up every bit of information they can get their hands on. The big

Figure 1.2
Ironically, this professional organizer's website is bogged down with too many navigation options. But Mandy Patinkin likes it.

problem is that much of the information that is presented is information that needs to be updated. And if too much information is presented, it is difficult to keep track of it all and keep it up-to-date. One reason people use the Web instead of more traditional media (such as a printed catalog) is to get up-to-date information. If a company's six-month-old winter catalog is more accurate than its website, you know that the website is emphasizing the wrong information.

- **Lack of focus.** The larger a site becomes, the more often it loses focus, and then it becomes apparent that its owner has tried to do too much with it. A site that is designed to be a store shouldn't be an online magazine. A site that is a help center for a company's products shouldn't get bogged down providing investor relations or financial information about the company. After all, when you need help getting your printer to work, the last thing you want to do is wade through menus of financial information to find the printer driver you need to download!

- **Search time hogs.** In the early days of websites, most users and designers would measure the success of a good website design in terms of how fast a home page or other critical pages would load. If, for example, a designer created a site with a home page that could load in two seconds, he might brag to his friends how great (and how useable) his website is. As information about how most users use the Web became available, this turned out to be a very deceptive metric. Certainly, web pages should load as quickly as possible, but what's really important is how much time it takes a user to find information on a website. Often, big websites are plagued with inefficiencies that make it really difficult to find information. A sure sign that a site is bloated is that it takes you many minutes to find a piece of information such as a company's email address, phone number, or physical address. Big websites often became very cumbersome because the designers don't often really think about the hierarchy of the information they need to present and arrange their site so that the most important information can be located first.

- **The "Where should I click?" syndrome.** A bloated site can be like a shared refrigerator in a group house occupied by three or more recent college grads. Everyone carves out a niche: "This is my ice cream" and

Figure 1.3
Lucky for you that the pages of this book can't flash like the eye-assaulting orange boxes on this site. The hyperactive display leaves you wondering where to start.

"Don't touch my tofu" labels litter the interior. On an overloaded website, instead of "Where's the mayonnaise?" the visitor wonders, "Where should I click?" The telltale signs are flashing graphics or scrolling text (see Figure 1.3); links to unrelated side businesses, partners, and affiliates; clutter; and chaos. For the visitor, the reaction may be stomach-turning. The only remedy may be to clean it out and start over.

- **Designed based on the org chart.** Businesses that don't stop to think about what visitors to their site might want fall back on one of the most common and ineffective web design strategies out there: Creating a website that mirrors the way they see themselves rather than how their customers see them. Then, when someone has the bright idea to put something on the site that visitors might want, the text or graphic or link gets wedged into a place it wasn't meant to go (see previous point). Wash, rinse, and repeat—the bloated site is born.

Figure 1.4
A big, bloated website like the IKEA site is plagued with many of the "big" website problems presented in this section.

WEBSITE BLOAT—THE IKEA WAY

Anyone who has ever shopped in an IKEA store knows how this innovative company has perfected the experience of shopping for furniture and home furnishings. IKEA, based in Sweden, has stores in many countries around the world, including about two dozen stores in the United States. In each of its stores, IKEA provides showcase rooms—from bathrooms and living rooms to children's playrooms—so that you can see firsthand how its products work together. The best part about the IKEA in-store experience is that you can easily find and purchase products without having to ask too many questions. The IKEA stores provide the perfect source for the do-it-yourself customer who needs to find inexpensive but practical solutions.

The IKEA website (**www.ikea.com**) is another matter entirely. It serves as the poster child for everything that can go bad with a big bloated site (see Figure 1.4). The site is very difficult to navigate and use to find products. Products are listed in many different areas of the site, and some products are available for purchase online but others aren't. There doesn't seem to be any logic behind what is offered for sale online and what isn't. Even the customer service people you can reach by using the company's 800 number seem to be completely confused by how the website works. The main product index on the site primarily lists the company's products by the products' name (in Swedish). Most customers who try to use the IKEA site to locate a product for purchase end up having to consult a Swedish dictionary or call the company to try to locate what they need.

After spending a few minutes using the IKEA site, it becomes apparent that it was designed by a committee who tried to put in every feature they could but missed the most important design principle—a good site needs to be easy to use and navigate. Before you get too involved with this chapter, try to spend a little time exploring the IKEA site, if you haven't already, and make a list of some of the things that trouble you about a big, bloated site like this. Keep this list handy because being aware of some of the aspects that can make a site boated and cluttered will help you keep your own site focused and running well.

The Small Site Philosophy

Small sites are resource friendly. They respect your time and budget. And more importantly, small sites respect your visitor's time—web surfers have notoriously short attention spans. Unfortunately, many people think that having a smaller site means "compromise" in the negative sense. Nothing could be further from the truth.

The driving design philosophy behind small sites is that you can do more with less. By focusing on what really matters— such as good design and navigation, well-written text, and high-impact graphics—you can create a website that contributes to your business or enterprise.

Small sites are resource friendly. You get the feeling that their owners respect your time and budget and, more important, that they respect your time—web surfers have notoriously short attention spans. Small sites also offer you a degree of *control* and the ability to continually improve—something that simply *cannot* be achieved when your website becomes bloated. Small sites are also much easier to maintain. As sites become larger, the time and resources required to keep them up-to-date increases exponentially.

While not necessarily a paragon of knock-out website *design,* I think the site for Jefferson City, Missouri–based Westside Dental (see Figure 1.5) is a great small site nonetheless. The site loads fast, has a delightfully whimsical tooth-shaped *W* as part of its logo, makes finding out the basics about the business easy, and provides three customer-oriented graphical links at the top of the page. There's no Flash movie of a patient getting a cleaning. We all know what that looks (and feels) like and don't care to relive it on a website. There's no online appointment scheduler. The phone handles that very well, thank you very much. Small sites like this one take care of the basics first by giving visitors what *they* want and eschewing the frills of website bloat.

Get Over the Fear of Smallness

A small, simple site need not be boring. If it meets the needs of your customers and potential customers, then it's not boring. As web design and usability guru Jakob Nielsen often asserts in his books and articles, visitors to your site spend most of their time on other websites. When they get to your site, they do not want to wait for a long Flash intro to finish, unravel your novel navigation scheme, decipher your clever marketing slogans, or wade through a mish-mash of disparate visual elements scattered across your home page.

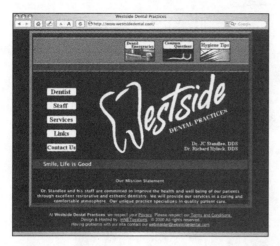

Figure 1.5
A Missouri dentist's website shows its patient
focus with links at the top of the page for
dental emergencies, common questions,
and hygiene tips.

Figure 1.6
The website skipintro.com pokes fun at overproduced and unnecessary introductory pages
with this meaningless example.

How Small Is Small?

In examining hundreds of websites for this book, one key issue that I continually had to consider was how small a site must be to still be considered a small site. Coming up with an actual definition for a small site turned out to be much more difficult than I first thought simply because there is such a wide range of websites with few design standards in place. In Chapter 2, I'll present some design standards that I think will help you better understand what the attributes of small sites are. In my exploration of model small sites, I did come up with a site that probably sets the record for being the smallest side on the Web. Take a look at this site, which is called guimp (**www.guimp.com**), and I think you'll agree (see Figure 1.7)! I'm not exactly holding it up as the model of the most practical site, but it does show you what can be done when you think really small.

When you design and build right, your small site will provide users with the kind of experience that makes them want to visit and return. *They'll also want to get to know your business better, which should be the real goal of your site.*

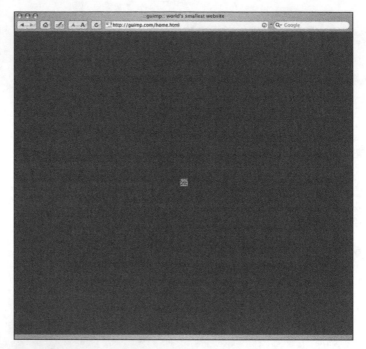

Figure 1.7
Introducing guimp—the world's smallest website!

You may think that without an artistic and splashy introductory page, visitors won't be impressed with your website and your business. In truth, people come to your site with a specific need or task in mind, so putting an extra page, or extra download time, or anything else between them and their goal will drive them away in frustration.

You may think that putting pictures and links to every product you sell on your home page will serve all your customers and potential customers in the most efficient way. Actually, a site without a clear visual hierarchy will confound many of those customers. You may think that building a site that includes every last word of your sparkling brochure copy will send untold customers and their dollars to your bottom line, but you would be wrong.

What really matters is not how cool your website is but how effectively it supports your business and how much it contributes to your bottom line. Your website should make your customers happy by saving them time and offering them products and services they can't easily find elsewhere. Your website is not just a showcase for your designer's creative talents but an essential sales and marketing channel.

Keep in mind that the novelty aspect of the Internet has long since worn off for most users. They are no longer impressed with Flash introductions or great animation. They now use the Internet as they would any other business tool—to get a job done quickly and efficiently. If you keep in mind that your customers probably don't want to waste time on your site and will appreciate an efficiently organized place to do business, a small and well-designed site will ultimately only benefit your business.

Does "Small" Mean "Puny?"

You might be uncomfortable with the notion of a small site because you might think such a site would give you a poor and anemic presence on the Web. That's not the kind of site I'm talking about. Just because you build a small site doesn't mean you can't have important features that you'll find on big sites, such as sections to purchase products, critical descriptions about your company's products or services, company support information, downloadable coupons or marketing materials, forms that let your visitors interact with your business, attractive and appropriate graphics, and so on.

Building small means leaving out marginal or excessive content—especially if you won't have time to keep it fresh and up-to-date. Successful small sites make a positive impact on visitors, but avoid overstating the size of your business with superfluous embellishments. Every piece of a small site must pass the business-benefit test: Does it save you the time you would spend on the phone or answering the same email over and over again? Does it save you money by replacing postage or faxing costs? Does it complement your other marketing efforts? Can your customers easily do what they want to do on your site?

Case Study: A Bloated and Confused Site

The Starbird Music website (Portland, Maine) illustrates how bloat prevents a site from being focused and accountable. Notice how the home page loudly beats the company's drum about its excellent location and all the brands of products it offers in its store (Figure 1.8). The site also illustrates a preoccupation with telling everything at the expense of effectively communicating anything. And the jumble of type above and below the four pictures, when viewed on the Web, is not one but two streams of moving text. All in all, a very confusing site.

TRYING TO LOOK BIG, ENDING UP BLOATED

Have you ever wondered how websites get so large and bloated in the first place?

Certainly the size and scope of the most popular websites—with a little help from media hype—has contributed to a larger-than-life view of the Web and all it offers. The largest and most frequently visited sites on the Web—Amazon, Yahoo, MSN, and AOL, just to name a few—are all exciting, dynamic, and money-making ventures for the companies that run them. All offer such a mind-boggling array of services, features, and pages that the average Web surfer has no hope (and probably no interest) in finding, figuring out, and using it all. The expanse of these high-profile sites has led to the false assumption that building big is the only way to succeed on the Web.

In the past, the people in charge of designing and building websites had little or no vested interest in making the sites really work for the people who use them. Imagine an engineer who doesn't like to drive designing your next car. Website designers and programmers can have a different agenda than that of your business. At times, their agenda might even be at odds with yours. But in today's hyper-competitive markets, you must understand the goals and needs of your online audience. And everyone who works on your site must understand it, too.

Another reason for website bloat is that many business people don't have a clear vision of what a useful, attractive, profit-producing site should look like. They therefore fall victim to the "If you don't know what to do, then do lots of things and hope some of them turn out right" approach.

If you don't see anything wrong with a bloated website, compare the following two scenarios. First, imagine going to your local hardware store to find a box of nails. You go up to the counter, you ask the clerk where the nails are, and the clerk tells you where to go look. This is the ideal experience, one you would likely get at a small, efficient store: good customer service, good organization, and quick and useful answers.

Now imagine that before you walk through the entrance of the store, a huge screen drops down in front of you and music starts playing. You hear a stirring commentary about the hardware store. Then a high-powered slide show about the store plays on the screen. You notice there's a button on the side of the screen that says, "Push this button to enter the store." As you ignore all of this nonsense and walk into the

Figure 1.8
Opening screen: What's going on here?

Let's now look at the site strictly from the point of view of the business. As an exercise, do your best to answer the following questions:

1. What is your initial impression of this website?

2. Does this site describe any of the store's benefits or any reasons you should you buy from it?

3. Who is the intended visitor to this website?

4. What action does Starbird Music want you to take?

5. How many navigation links does the site offer you? Which links do you want to click?

6. What kind of impression does this website, and this business, make on you?

7. How can Starbird Music evaluate the success of this website?

Got your answers? Let's go back to the questions, one by one, so you can see why I asked them:

1. **What is your initial impression of this website?**

   I can't imagine that you found it delightful, impressive, or confidence-building. If you put yourself in the frame of mind of a potential customer—a piano buyer—your impression could be decidedly worse. Since I personally know a lot of piano players, I know that piano players in general are rather fussy people." Would a fussy person warm up to a website that, to put it mildly, has little focus?

2. **Does this site describe any of the store's benefits or any reasons you should you buy from it?**

   Maybe it does, but I can't find those benefits or reasons. I have worked professionally with hundreds of businesses helping them find and communicate benefits and reasons to attract customers. Did you find any benefits or reasons that you didn't have to strain your brain to come up with?

3. **Who is the intended visitor to this website?**

   The knee-jerk answer, of course, is people who are interested in pianos. But look more closely. At the top, you see the logos of five different piano and organ manufacturers. It seems to me that the only person who would really be interested in that is the sales rep for the one of the companies that isn't represented...so she could get a little free exposure for her company, too. The problem is that the site doesn't directly address, or indirectly satisfy, the questions most on the mind of the prospective customer: Is this a good store that has its act together? Will I be treated well? Can I get what I'm looking for here? Will I be take care of after the sale? Is it worth my time and trouble to come by and visit, or even pick up the phone and call?

4. **What action does Starbird Music want you to take?**

   Starbird does ask you to visit the store or send an email. It says so, right at the bottom of the page. But why would you want to visit or email? Doing so would only benefit Starbird—or you, if you were just about ready to buy a piano. That leaves out a lot of people. My point is that this site offers no service that would bring along a barely interested customer to the level of a warm prospect, nor does it give current customers any action to take to stay in a relationship with the store. Look at all those missed opportunities!

---

store, you notice five clerks standing just inside the door, all yelling at you all at once. "Brooms!" "Mops!" "Sponges!" "Shovels!" "Electrical parts!"

So ask yourself, "Which store would I prefer?"

Sadly, most bloated sites are a lot like this outrageous hardware store. Sites often have unnecessary, overproduced audiovisual presentations that play automatically when you first arrive. Get past that and you encounter multiple graphics and text blocks on the home page competing for your attention (see Figure 1.8). Try to find what you need on the site and you find yourself frustrated because it seems you are going around in circles.

5. **How many navigation links does the site offer you? Which links do you want to click?**

   I counted 16. I'm still deciding which ones to click.

6. **What kind of impression does this website, and this business, make on you?**

   If it's a good impression, you're easily impressed. The site is not business-like, focused, customer-oriented...and that's bad for business.

7. **How can Starbird Music evaluate the success of this website?**

   This, perhaps, is the biggest problem of all. Because there's no "trackable" action that the site asks the visitor to take, there's no objective way to measure its success. You can send an email, but that is hardly meaningful by itself. As a "necessary evil," this site earns its keep. But as a productive, profitable part of the business, it's got a long way to go.

Website Bloat and What It Means

It's not always politically correct (that is, safe) to criticize your company's website, especially if it looks cool and includes everything under the sun. But at the water cooler and in closed-door meetings, the real truth comes out:

- *Marketing professionals* are frustrated by a lack of control. With a large, bloated site, it's tough or impossible to get any meaningful results or track how effective the site is. What's worse, every little change becomes a major production. It becomes expensive and difficult to change the site, so things stay the way they are. Or, additions to the site end up being more of the same—more complexity, less focus, and greater sprawl.

- *Financial professionals* are frustrated by a lack of accountability. Each month brings a new slew of invoices from designers, programmers, writers, web hosting services, and—often—a host of high-priced consultants.

- *Sales professionals* are frustrated by a lack of user-friendliness. Instead of being their comrade-in-arms, the bloated site is their enemy. They can't use the site to make their jobs easier because they know customers visiting the site get confused and lose interest in buying the product. Pleas to make the site more supportive of the sales process just seem to fall on deaf ears because of the difficulty of making changes to the site.

Many people secretly think of a bloated site as an out-of-control monster, something that has to be tolerated as a cost of doing business rather than enthusiastically embraced as the technological breakthrough that it represents.

Follow the Leaders, But Don't Imitate Them

Large websites have much to teach us about how to design and maintain a small website, but the doctrine of success-through-size is not one of them. One way big sites lead the way for small sites is by setting the standards for how we expect a website to behave.

The best example is the shopping cart, the virtual collection of items you're planning to purchase when browsing an online store. The virtual shopping cart metaphor succeeds online because it most clearly mimics the function of its offline counterpart—and, more important, because it's used by the world's largest online store, Amazon.com (see Figure 1.9).

Figure 1.9
Amazon.com and other large, popular websites set standards for website design by endorsing conventions such as the ubiquitous "shopping cart" metaphor for e-commerce sites.

Other examples include labeling the button that starts a search with obvious terms like "Search" or "Find," rather than the more generic "Go" or "Submit," or using short descriptive words or phrases for links rather than the cryptic and alarmingly pervasive "Click Here."

The Problem with "Click Here"

You'll be hard-pressed to find the words "click here" describing a hypertext link on any well-designed and successful large site, but their appearance on a small site is a sure tip-off that the site exhibits other symptoms of bloat as well. What's worse, without sufficient context, a link with the words "click here" can cause a customer to fear they'll be put on a spam list by clicking since "click here" is a link often found in spam e-mails.

Here are a few words of wisdom from leading web design experts on the problem with "click here."

"A common mistake that many Web authors make in creating links in body text is using the 'here' syndrome. The here syndrome is the tendency to create links with a single highlighted word (here) and to describe the link somewhere else in the text.

"Because links are highlighted on the Web page, the links visually 'pop out' more than the surrounding text (or 'draw the eye' in graphic design lingo). Your readers will see the link first, before reading the text. Try creating links this way. Close your eyes, open them quickly, pick a 'here' at random, and then see how long it takes you to find out what the 'here' is for." — *Laura Lemay's Teach Yourself Web Publishing with HTML 4 in 14 Days* "...don't move readers through hypertext by telling them where things are. Links are obvious to all but the most inexperienced web surfers, and telling users 'More information is available here' or 'To see the movie, click here' assumes they know nothing about how their browser works. Leave those tutorials for the instruction manual and help pages. Don't describe the technology, and don't be condescending. Give your readers the context they need to make their decisions." — *Jeffrey Veen, Hot Wired Style* "The oldest web design rule is to avoid using 'Click Here' as the anchor text for a hypertext link. There are two reasons for this rule. First, only mouse-using visitors do in fact click, whereas disabled users or users with a touchscreen or other alternative device don't click. Second, the words 'Click' and 'Here' are hardly information-carrying and, as such, should not be used as a design element that attracts the user's attention." — *Jakob Nielsen, Designing Web Usability*

While some big companies make running a large site look easy, keep in mind that they also commit considerable amounts of time and money to making sure the myriad features they provide to their users pay off, from scrutinizing the placement, size, and wording of individual elements on the site to analyzing the path each user follows through the site. You can do the same on your small site, but remember that some tricks employed by the major players on the Web won't scale down, and remain profitable, for a small site operator on a budget.

Features Used by Large Sites That Could Benefit Small Sites

A website that's too large and complex for the business that supports it is a recipe for bloat. Consider the following tools, services, and features employed by large sites, the resources they consume, and some suggested small-site alternatives.

Using a Content Management System (CMS)

Most large websites are managed through a Web-based interface that stores website content in a database, allowing multiple people to add, edit, or delete content from the site. Popular commercial CMS include Vignette and Interwoven. Open-source choices include Zope, eZ Publish, Midgard, and Pagetool.

Downside: Without investing the time to create a workflow and style guidelines for everyone using the system, your website can quickly devolve into chaos. And while many CM systems are free to install and use, setup and customization fees can erode their benefit.

Small Site Alternative: Build your site modularly by reusing small pieces of content with the built-in features of HTML. Keep printouts of your web pages in a binder and use old-fashioned pen-and-paper records to track what's on your site's pages, who changed them, and when. I'll come back to easy, small-site strategies for maintaining and updating your site in Chapter 10.

Providing Large Audio or Video Files

You may have a large product demo, movie, or audio file that you want to place on your website for the benefit of your visitors.

Downside: Without creating instructions for the required plug-ins or helper applications, you will find yourself answering emails from users who can't view the file. And large files can consume costly disk space and download quotas on your web server.

Small Site Alternative: Create a low-bandwidth alternative, either as an animated GIF, DHTML slide show, or series of web pages that visitors to your website can view within their browser.

Creating a Members-Only Section

Perhaps you have some exclusive content or files or other materials that you want to protect. A password-protected section of your website might seem to be the way to go.

Downside: Your registered users will forget their password or will attempt to access your site with a browser that the system was not designed for. You, or your web designer, will spend time troubleshooting the problems, erasing the profit potential for this feature.

Small Site Alternative: Screen requests for exclusive content by requiring interested site visitors to submit a simple mail-to form, then direct them to an FTP download for the content they desire.

Accepting Advertising

Perhaps the enticement of adding a new revenue stream to your site has you contemplating adding advertisements.

Downside: Advertisers expect measurable results, information you may not be able to provide without installing and maintaining an expensive ad tracking system on your web server. (This may also require additional personnel to manage the reports and perform analysis on the data.) Also, web ads come in specific sizes and are best placed in familiar positions on a web page. If you're site wasn't designed to accommodate ads, you may have to spend time and money to redesign it for such a purpose. Finally, the ads you receive may be poorly designed, and you may feel compelled to create a customized ad to satisfy the advertiser.

Small Site Alternative: If you're committed to exploiting this facet of Web-based revenue, consider selling a sponsorship on your site by placing the logos of one or two complementary businesses or organizations on a few of the key pages.

My point is not that adding the advanced functionality to your site is a waste of time and money. It is that your website should be focused and adhere to some basic guidelines before you consider adding on. Automated tools are useful, and there's a time and place for them. But they can consume resources and may be overkill. I'll come back to these ideas in Chapters 9 and 10 when I discuss designing an easy-to-maintain site and what to do when you've outgrown your small site.

The key challenge for the Web in the twenty-first century is one of bloat. Bloated sites lack focus for the people who visit them, and they lack meaningful, trackable results for the businesses that run them. They often end up being a source of expense rather than profits. A bloated website that's too big for the business that supports it is difficult to update and costly to maintain, making it nearly impossible to see the benefit of the investment.

By committing to building a small site and avoiding website bloat, you'll find it easier to improve your site incrementally, and test features such as special offers, headlines, and prices. In the end, you'll have more control, increased profits, lower costs, and fewer hassles.

Summary

In this chapter you learned about the issues surrounding bloated sites. You learned that bloated sites are ineffective because they offer too much and do too little. Bloated sites suffer myriad problems that affect both your business and your site visitors. They're hard to use and hard to maintain. They drain resources from your business, turn off visitors, and prevent you from reaching new customers with your site.

You also learned the antidote to bloat: the Small Site philosophy, which is that you should do more with less because more is not necessarily better when it comes to your website. Small sites are not boring, puny, or compromised in any way. Rather, they represent your business online in a way that respects your resources and your visitors' time and interests. Successful small sites turn visitors into customers.

WHAT MAKES A GREAT SMALL SITE?

- Learn what the basic components are for a small site—the essential qualities and attributes.

- Learn what to keep, what to leave out, and how to tell if your site is already bloated.

- Learn the basic design techniques for creating small sites.

After reading Chapter 1, you should have a good understanding of why building a big site is not always the best approach. You should also understand about the advantages that small sites can provide, such as better focus, less clutter, and more and better details in the areas where users can appreciate them the most. Let's dig a little deeper into the small site model to see what works. As I mentioned in Chapter 1, small sites can incorporate many of the features found in large sites without becoming bloated. But there's more to making a great site than just attending to the small details of web publishing, such as how to label your shopping cart and search function. Successful small sites should also get high marks in the broader qualities and attributes of what the experts call a website's "user experience."

Creating a Great User Experience

A great small site provides its visitors with a great user experience. That means a site should be easy to understand, functional without being overwhelming, and well organized. And it should be free of the trappings of bloat—focusing on its audience's needs rather than on adding the latest bell, whistle, or doodad.

The small site for Winslow and Associates, a San Francisco–based event planning and consulting firm, gets the user experience right in a lot of ways. The home page (see Figure 2.1) offers just the right balance

Figure 2.1
A clean and useful home page for Winslow and Associates, a San Francisco-based event planning and consulting firm.

of graphics, text, and navigation. The easy-to-spot boldface phone number encourages visitors to use the phone to get the latest information. The image on the right-hand side of the page cycles through logos and photos of recent projects and clients. Reiterating the menu choice that takes the visitor to subpages on the Winslow & Associates site is a subhead in the tan bar under the logo (see Figure 2.2). A bullet list of anchor links summarizes the page's subsections.

The site for CryptoMetrics, a New York–based "security software solution provider," lies on the other end of the user experience spectrum (see Figure 2.3 and Figure 2.4). The home page features a mediocre Flash animation of floating industry terminology and buzzwords, but no plain English explanation of what the company does and no navigation (which shows up only after you "enter" the "site").

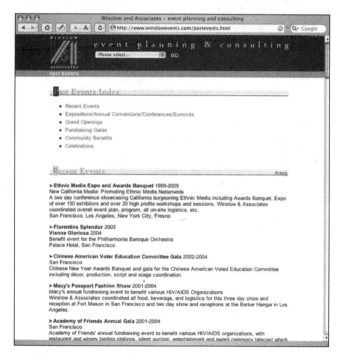

Figure 2.2
A Winslow & Associates site subpage.

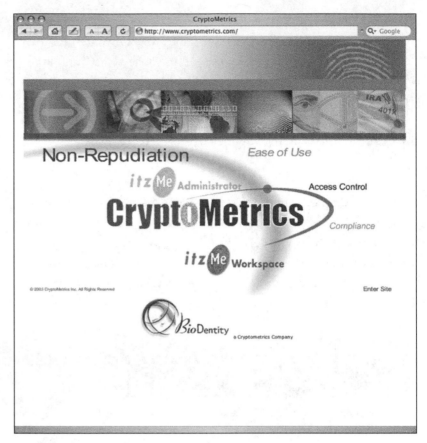

Figure 2.3
The cryptic home page for CryptoMetrics. Enter site? How did you
know that's what I want to do?

The following list includes the user experience attributes that are most
important to making your small site successful:

- **Providing the best context.** This involves giving visitors to your
  site clear cues about how to use it and what to expect from it. (In
  other words, your customer should never get lost in your website.)

- **Providing good task orientation.** Visitors to your site must be able
  to easily find and do what they came to do. They should never
  have to work too hard or spend too much time finding something
  that is important.

- **Maintaining hierarchy or using organizational guidelines.**
  Good structure and organization can greatly help your visitors
  understand the relative importance of various parts of your
  website. In setting up the structure for your site, you should think

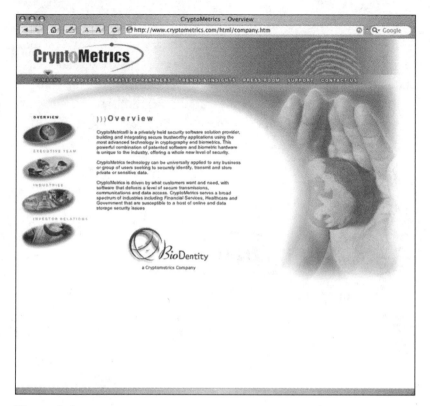

Figure 2.4
A subpage on the CryptoMetrics site has the fingerprints of some well-meaning but misguided web designer all over it.

carefully about the various paths the visitor to your site will encounter. Everything should be in its proper place and nothing should be too difficult to find. If a visitor needs to click too many links to get access to an important feature, your site likely has become too complex with too much hierarchy.

Let's look at the key small site attributes in more detail.

Give Your Visitors Good Context

Context is crucial to creating a useful experience for visitors. It helps people relate to your message and know what to expect as they use your website. The key to providing context on your website lies in giving visitors clear directions and explanations about where they are on your site, where they can go, what they can do when they get there, and how they can get back on track if something goes wrong.

As the old adage about storytelling goes, first tell them what you're going to tell them, then tell them, then tell them what you told them. Giving your audience some perspective on your message through repetition strengthens what you have to say, and it helps your audience focus on your key points and how your business can benefit them. Websites, like stories, can have a narrative structure—links, buttons, and navigation that propel the experience (see Figure 2.5).

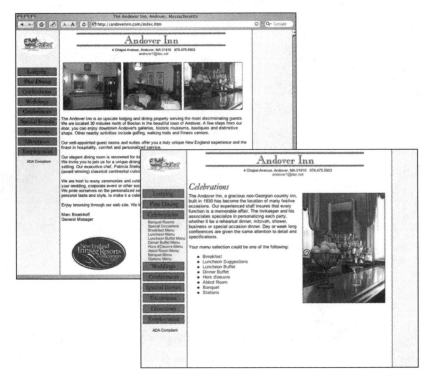

Figure 2.5
On the Andover Inn home page, clicking the blue button labeled "Celebrations" loads a page with corresponding headline and secondary links. Navigation and page headlines work together to give visitors a sense of where they are on your site.

Successful small sites give users context by maintaining a consistent layout and color scheme; adhering to well-delineated areas for content, navigation, and marketing/advertising messages; and presenting information with engaging, benefit-oriented headlines, useful labels, and error messages. The bloated site, on the other hand, mixes ad-like animated graphics and logos with content, changes its look and navigation from page to page, and uses murky or inconsistent language in its headlines and text. Visitors to bloated sites get confused, give up, and leave.

Make It Easy for Users to Do What They Came to Do

Your site should provide good task orientation, namely, highlighting tasks so they're easy to find and use. A visit to your website can— among other things—make a phone call unnecessary and save postage. Successful small sites are focused on enabling actions that save time and money when done via the Web. Notice how the navigation choices on the website for New Mexico attorneys Steven Granberg and Gail Stewart (see Figure 2.6) are presented in straightforward,

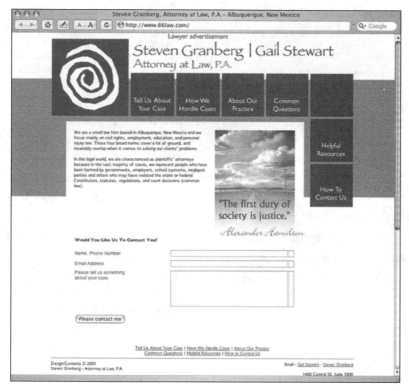

Figure 2.6
The navigation choices on this attorney's website are clearly geared toward the common tasks of clients and prospective clients.

action-orient language: "Tell Us About Your Case," "How We Handle Cases," and so on. Contrast that with the navigation choices on the home page for Sweet Tulip—"Baby" (baby what?), "Publicity" (their word for it), and "Wholesale" (is that me?)—which demonstrate a business-centric rather than visitor-centric way of organizing a website (see Figure 2.7).

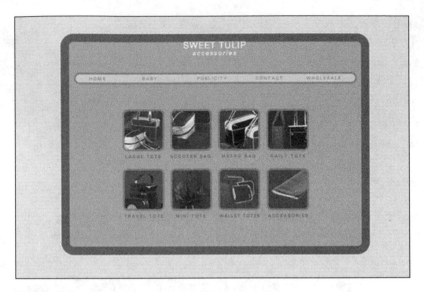

Figure 2.7
On sweettulip.com, the navigation choices in the light-colored horizontal bar reflect how the business sees itself, not how visitors might use its website.

Bloated sites neglect the needs of their visitors. The resources for doing the desired tasks may be there, but finding them amid the overwhelmingly complex and slow-loading presentations may prove too challenging for first-time visitors to the site. Or the bloated site may be poorly organized or hard to update so that keeping up with customers' needs is too costly, time consuming, or complex.

How can you know what visitors to your site will want to do? Your website visitors' needs are probably more basic than you think. Think about the questions you get from customers offline—by phone, mail, or in person—and how you could answer them online:

- When are you open (or when is your next appearance if you're a performer/author)?

- What is the nature of your business?

- Can I download a new menu, catalog, price list, or instruction manual?

- Can I get a price quote on your mailing list or be placed on your waiting list?

- Who's in charge of returns, new accounts, sales, or complaints?

- Where can I buy your products?

If you can't come up with a list like this for your business, keep a pad of paper next to your phone or ask your salespeople what they're hearing from customers.

Altogether, the user actions on your website give it a purpose—a reason why someone would visit it just once or visit it once a week—and they help you differentiate your business from your competitors.

Create and Maintain Good Hierarchy

Because people prefer to browse, search, and scan the contents of websites rather than read every single word, a successful small site should be organized to give visitors a quick, structured overview. Using a hierarchical structure lets them get a little bit of information, and then they'll (hopefully!) dig a little deeper if they want more.

Think back to your middle school English class. Do you remember the Roman numeral headings, subheads, and topic sentences? Before you began writing that book report or essay, your teacher likely asked you to turn in an outline. Stripped of its logos, colorful text treatments and images, a website should be a lot like an outline, an orderly presentation of what's the most important thing to know about the company it represents, what's the second most important, and so forth. A successful small site keeps things in proportion with a hierarchical structure of most to least important that lets users get as little or as much information as they want from your site without becoming overwhelmed.

The textual content of your site has to be balanced with appropriate visual cues. Don't fall into the trap of giving your visitor too much text to read in a single page. On the other hand, you need to be mindful of the bloat that can be created by having too many images. Communicating effectively on the Web is all about achieving the right balance. The navigation and graphical elements on your site should be sized and placed on your web pages to convey their relative importance to one another. Text should be concise and presented in easy-to-read short lines and paragraphs. A bloated website is full of heavy text blocks and lacks an easily discernible organization. The navigation can't be distinguished from the content, the content from the ads, the ads from the navigation.

On the site for Baseline Technologies (see Figure 2.8), what appears to be important content is relegated to a cramped gray sidebar on the left side of the home page, while little more than a dull-looking block of

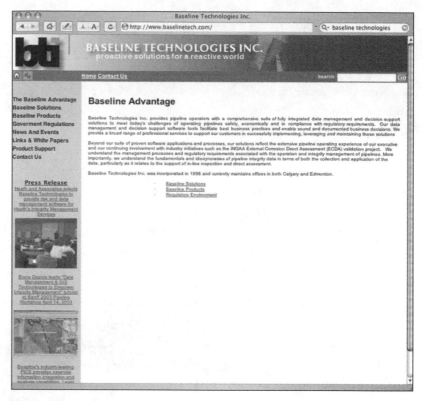

Figure 2.8
With much of its home page content on the left sidebar, this site presents a lopsided hierarchy.

text is offered in the page layout's main area. On the Colt Refining website, photos, graphics, and text are balanced and arranged in a way that improves the user experience (see Figure 2.9).

If your site's outline isn't really clear and structurally sound, it's likely that your site is difficult to navigate. Every investment you make in fine-tuning your outline will likely pay off considerably with the praise and (hopefully) increased business you get from your site.

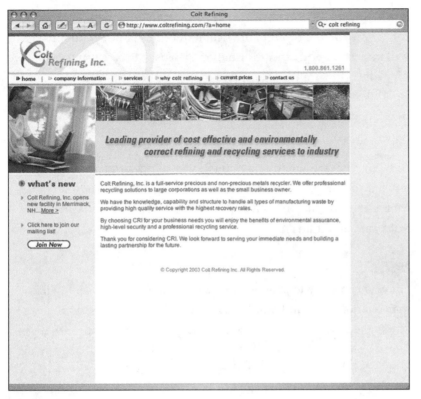

Figure 2.9
Fine points like a color-coordinated logo, phone number, and "what's new" bullet; short paragraphs; and a simple tagline callout make the Colt Refining website easy to scan and use.

Basic Components of a Small Site

With the qualities of a successful site in mind, you may already have a good idea about what you're going to put on yours. But the most difficult decisions may be how to decide what to leave out. If you put everything you desire on your website, you'll end up with a bloated mess.

Building and maintaining a website requires a kind of discipline not required by other forms of publishing. The ease with which you can add something to your website can lead to an "anything goes" mentality. *But just because you can doesn't mean you should.*

Printed publications such as newsletters, catalogs, and brochures are constrained by the cost and physical limitations of paper and ink, as well as postage and other distribution expenses. Broadcasters have time limits, transmitter range, and federal standards within which to work. Web publishing has few constraints. Websites can expand indefinitely, and many do. Web pages hang around long after their creators have forgotten their original purpose.

To help you determine if something is worth including on your site, let's look at some of the components of a small site and how they contribute to (or detract from) how your site provides context, enables tasks, and maintains hierarchy.

Logo

Put your company logo on your website. I know, it's a no-brainer, but there's a right way and many wrong ways. Here are some guidelines: Match the color and composition of your website logo with how it looks in other contexts—your signs, letterhead, advertisements, pens—to reassure visitors that they've arrived at the website they were expecting. Don't make it spin, or flash, or slide into view. A slow connection to your site can stall before your special effects load, so optimize your logo graphic so it loads quickly. Keep the logo relatively small and discreetly placed near the upper-left corner of your web pages (see Figure 2.10 and Figure 2.11). Your logo also can double as a shortcut link back to your home page, so the upper-left placement reinforces the mental map in your visitors' minds that clicking your logo takes them back to the beginning of your site. Elements on a web page work best when they adhere to an inverse relationship between size and frequency; elements that appear on every page should be smaller than an item that appears on it only once.

Figure 2.10.
Putting the logo in the lower-right corner might work if this were a catalog or brochure layout. But on the Web, you run the risk that people with small monitors won't see it.

Figure 2.11
A better way—neatly tuck the logo in the upper-left corner of your pages. This one goes one better, including the business's location.

Navigation

Consistent links and buttons on your site can help visitors understand how your site is structured and where they are within it. Whether your navigation runs across the top of the screen or along the side, make sure its size, color, and placement are consistent on all the pages in your website. The number of navigation items to include on your pages differs depending on the nature of your business and your website. Eight to 12 seems to be the generally accepted maximum; in many cases, the fewer the better. Once you're into the double digits, you run the risk of weighing down your pages with too many options. If your site consists of sections—even if they are one-page sections— change your primary navigation to highlight the navigational element for the page or section the visitor is currently looking at or browsing within (see Figure 2.12).

Figure 2.12
A subtle color change in the primary navigation (top) indicates the current section of the site. On the murus.com site shown here, a small arrowhead marks the page's location in the site structure.

Splash Screens

Whether it's a high-energy, animated Flash commercial or just a static logo or other graphic that "sets the mood" for your website, splash screens are usually unnecessary (see Figure 2.13). Unless your site visitors come to your website to be entertained or surprised, a splash screen will prevent them from getting on with the real reason they are visiting your site. Still not convinced? One of the fastest-selling consumer electronic devices of the last few years is the digital video recorder, which—among its other benefits—lets people skip TV commercials. Why put a commercial on your website?

Figure 2.13
Splash screens aren't all bad (but most are). A consultant who advises American businesses on expanding to Japan makes good use of a splash page to offer a language choice to visitors before they proceed to the home page (top). Without giving a reason why its home page features nothing more than a logo, the website for a nanny placement firm presents a different choice to visitors: stay or go.

Splash screens often seem to fill a void left by a web designer who hasn't a clue what to put on a site's home page. Web designers who know better often talk about what should go "above the fold" on a web page, meaning the elements that should appear on the screen with no need to scroll down or click through. ("Above the fold" originated in the newspaper industry, where the most prominent place for headlines and articles is the top half of the front page.) Your logo, site navigation, and a short tagline that describes your business should always appear "above the fold" on your home page.

Page Titles, Filenames, Headlines, and Link Text

Successful sites include the basic browser guideposts—link text, page titles, and headlines—to reassure visitors that where they ended up is where they intended to go. Links on your site that do something other than lead to another page—for example, links that lead to another site or open another window—should be annotated to let your site's visitors know what to expect. If the link downloads a file, make sure it indicates the file type with an icon and file size. If the link creates an email message, use the email address for the link rather than the person's name.

Site Map

A site map is a condensed list of the major sections and subsections of your site on one page. Site maps can be a big help for visitors to medium and large sites, especially those without a site-search function. Site maps also can give your visitors another way to see how your site is organized (see Figure 2.14), and search-engine spiders can quickly index all the pages on your site by following links from your site map. But beware: Site maps can easily end up neglected and out-of-sync with newer pages added to the site, leaving visitors with out-of-date links and old information.

Figure 2.14
Site maps like this provide an overview of your site's organization, but they can be a site maintenance challenge.

Contact Us Page

Whether you want to collect sales leads, provide a free quote, or sign up people for a mailing list, start using your site to interact with your customers and potential customers. The "Contact Us" link that you provide can be a key piece of your business strategy. This link can provide information about who the key players are in your company, where you are located, who is involved in your distribution network, and various "help" options. If structured in a compelling way, it can be a major way of reaching out to your customers for feedback. Interactive feedback forms can be set up as mini applications. They have inputs, logic, and outputs, and the way each component of the "application" is handled can dictate the usefulness of the form for you and your site visitors.

If you do provide such a feature, make sure that you have the resources and a system set up to respond to the email or form-based inquiries that you receive. There is nothing more frustrating for a visitor or potential customer than to visit a site, send in an inquiry through a "Contact Us" feature, and then never receive a response.

FAQs

Use your site to save your customers a phone call, and yourself the time spent answering the same questions over and over again. Set up a feedback loop to put questions you get offline—that is, by phone, by mail, or in person—and put the answers on your website.

Map

If you have lots of walk-in traffic or are in a hard-to-find location, a map and a picture of your building can quickly address the needs of customers who want to pay you a visit.

Mission Statement

Few visitors come to your site looking for a little light reading, so your mission statement will probably find a limited audience. However, if it can support the task of certain users—making a donation to your organization or choosing to do business with you over a competitor, then your mission statement has a place on your website. You can increase the likelihood that your mission statement will be read if it's only three to four sentences.

"Under Construction" Page

The tireless, animated construction worker with the shovel has had his fifteen minutes of Web fame. If you have to post a temporary page for your site, or even just a notice on one page that's not done yet, be sure to include a date by which you plan to launch the site or update the page. That gives visitors an idea of when to return to the site for the information they were seeking, and they just might bookmark your site and come back.

Designing Small Websites

As a designer of small sites and the author of this book, the first challenge I originally encountered was determining what exactly is a small site. It's easy to point out large sites simply because they really stand out and they are clumsy and difficult to use, as you learned in Chapter 1. We've all had the experience of trying to use a site on which so much product and company information is provided that we can't seem to find anything we really want. Locating small sites might seem more like trying to spot small birds in the forest—you can hear them and you know they are all around you but you have to really scan the canopy of the trees to find them.

Small sites also can't easily be defined based on a specific web page count. I've often encountered sites that provide only a few pages but are so disorganized, difficult to navigate, and poorly designed that they suffer from the maladies of big and bloated sites. As a starting point, I can, however, suggest some guidelines that you can use to help you locate and design small sites.

The Most Basic Small Site Can Be a Single-Page Site

Creating an effective single-page site for a business might seem like a real challenge (and it is!), but it can be done. As you can imagine, a single-page site needs to be really focused, and it needs to provide basic company information such as the type of business (does it offer products or services or both?), contact information (address, phone number, fax, and email), a photo (if appropriate for the business), and some type of call to action. A single-page site needs to function like an ad in the yellow pages, where space is at a premium and every word and image really counts. In general, you'll find that single-page sites often work well for businesses that are small and local and provide a highly targeted set of products or services.

As an example, let's assume you are a real estate agent in a mid-size town in the Midwest. Your primary goal should be to get new prospective clients to call you. You don't likely need a site that lists every single property that you have for sale (or ones that other agencies have for sale). What you likely need is a good "call to action" site that provides the information that is unique about your specialty and approach. If you try to provide too much information on your site, potential clients could get confused and turned off and never send you an email or pick up the phone and call you.

Small Sites Can Have Multiple Pages

You might find that a single-page site could work for the type of business that you have, but in most cases you'll simply need more pages to get out your message. This is especially true if you have a national or international business or if your business offers a range of products and/or services. The trick with sites that have multiple pages is to not let them get out of hand.

So how many pages is too many? It's difficult to come up with a hard and fast number. I find that a good easy-to-manage range is somewhere between 5 and 20 pages, although I have seen sites that provide more pages and still do a good job at operating small with good focus. As you work through this book, you'll encounter a number of sites that provide good models of small sites that use multiple pages. As you think about your site, it's important to not focus too much on counting pages but rather on determining the elements that you really need. Don't be afraid to leave out elements that aren't critical. For example, if you have a company that sells and ships metal bar stools, it might be okay to use multiple pages so that you can display all of the contact and ordering information, a list and short description of the products that you have (with sizing dimensions), information about your quality service and products, a simple shopping cart so that customers can order, samples of finishes and color swatches, and so on. What you likely don't need is Flash graphics that show how your bar stools swivel around. Leave this kind of junk for the big and bloated sites (your competitors!).

Small Sites Have Simple Navigation Devices

Whether your small site consists of a single page or multiple pages, you need simple and easy-to-use navigation devices. Using a website is all about navigation. The faster a user can find information, the less time they will need to spend and the more they will get the impression that your site is tight, focused, and reliable. This sends out the message that you know what you are doing and that you have a solid business.

With small sites, you really need to avoid what I call the "sins of navigation:"

- Using a complicated navigation device when a simple one will do.
- Using inappropriate metaphors as navigation "controllers." Ersatz radio tuning dials and VCR faceplates are common examples that may have seemed like a good idea at the time but aren't.
- Using any other cumbersome graphics as navigation devices.
- Using cumbersome phrases or industry terminology.

- Using multiple links to get somewhere the user can get with one link or action.

- Having dead-end links. (How many sites have you used where you can't return to the home page or another critical page?)

- Requiring users to pass their mouse over an unlabeled icon (or worse, a blank area of the screen) in order to reveal the navigation choices.

- Using pop-up windows as navigation bridges.

- Using Flash or a Java applet to generate the navigation images after the rest of the page loads.

If your site needs to be a little larger than you want it to be ideally because you have a lot of critical information to display, it's better to have more pages and keep your navigation devices really simple than to try to use fewer pages with complicated navigation devices.

Small Sites Can Have Simple Menus

If your site has enough pages or complexity that it needs a structured navigation device, a simple menu structure is fine. Avoid falling into the trap of providing too many menu options because this will make your site look cumbersome. The goal here is to arrange the overall features of your site into a small set of categories (five to eight or fewer). Here are some examples of menu categories for a typical site that offers products for sale:

Home

Shop for products

Product specials

Contact us

Information on shipping/customer service

Company/product FAQ

Testimonials or company guarantees

If your site seems small and focused in its structure and organization, it will be easy to use.

Small Sites Don't Include Time-Wasting Graphics

It's true that a good picture is worth a thousand words, but the reality is that most graphics on sites don't offer a lot. With most sites, the graphics simply make the site slow to load, difficult to navigate, and appear much bigger than it really is. Graphics can also be time consuming and expensive to create unless you have a lot of artistic talent to draw on. Instead of designing a small site by creating an assortment of images and then trying to incorporate text around the graphics, use the opposite approach. Images are used as punctuation and focal points to help direct the user's attention to critical issues and areas of the site.

Small Sites Provide Easy to Update Information

Designing and creating a site is only half of the battle. A good small site is designed so that it can be updated quickly and easily. The reality is that most businesses don't have the time to regularly update their sites. Here is the most common issue I run into with websites: I'll use a search engine such as Google to locate a company who offers a set of products I need to research or purchase. I'll then visit the site and try to find what I am looking for. After wasting a bit of time, I'll call up the company and speak with a customer service person only to hear the following: "Our site hasn't been updated in a while so the product you are looking for isn't listed but we do have it." When this happens, I'm tempted to send the company a message: "Thanks. Next time I'll use the yellow pages!"

Smart designers understand this frustration and thus design small websites so they don't fall into this trap. If you have information about products and services that you know you won't be able to regularly update, don't include it on your site. Instead, include a section that tells the user to call or email your company to find out more information. If you include incomplete information or information that hasn't been updated about your products and services, you'll never know if you lose a sale because a customer can't find what they're looking for. Don't leave such an important aspect of your business and website to chance.

Small Sites Are Great at Outsourcing

Whoever said that the best sites are ones that do everything on their own is dead wrong. Smart designers of small sites realize that the Internet is full of great resources that can be used to help build and support a website. For example, if you want to sell products on your site, you really don't need to build your own shopping cart. You can create a Yahoo! Store instead. Using sites like PayPal and Network for Good to collect payments for intangible goods like memberships, subscriptions, or donations is easier than setting up your own e-commerce engine and online credit card merchant account. Google offers services for creating a site search and placing small text ads on your site. Using MapQuest or Expedia (among others), you can put accurate maps and driving directions on your site. Topica and Yahoo will host your email list, as will dozens of other companies that specialize in email marketing so you don't have to. The list of specialty third-party services goes on and on, from audio/video and database hosting to live customer service chat applications and translating your site content into other languages.

A Small Site Can Have a Shopping Cart

Shopping carts don't necessarily have to be features provided by only big sites. As popular as big mall stores are, people still love to shop in small, focused stores. If you have a business that offers a unique set of products, there's no reason you can't sell your products on your site by using a very simple shopping cart. A good small site example is David Stephen Menswear (see Figure 2.15).

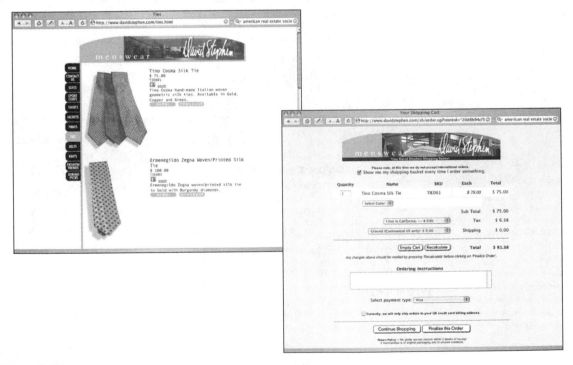

Figure 2.15
The navigation on the David Stephen Menswear site (left) provides quick access to online wares. The shopping cart pages (right) offer just the basic tools for completing the transaction.

Shopping carts can get very complicated because on many sites that provide them, all kinds of complicated features are included in the design. If you have a small business with a small set of products, there's no reason for this. All you need is a shopping cart that provides these basic features:

- Allows the user to select a product and add it to the cart

- Allows the user to delete items from the cart

- Allows the user to change quantities once an item has been added to the cart

- Allows the user to review all of the items that have been added to the cart

- Allows the user to check out with as few steps as possible

Small Sites Can Provide Catalog Pages

Because small websites should be designed to stay small, they don't need to list all products and services (just as long as this is made clear to the customer). Instead of setting up an elaborate database that provides information on all of a company's products and services, a smart small site can simply include catalog pages the user can download. Using PDF files, this is quick, easy, and inexpensive to do. The advantage of this approach is you won't gunk up your site trying to display too much product information and you can have more control of the visual presentation of your production and service information.

After reviewing hundreds of small-site examples for this book, I'm here to tell you that there is no small site poster child. In a way, a good small site is in the eye of the beholder (the visitor) and the business that runs it. The people who use your site don't care how big or how small it is as long as it loads quickly, presents an easy-to-understand experience, and lets them get the information they want or do what they came to the site to do with minimal hassle. Your goals as a business owner with a small site should fit hand-in-hand with the hopes and expectations of your visitors. An easy-to-use site that loads quickly should, by definition, be inexpensive to build and require limited effort to maintain.

Summary

In this chapter, you learned that a great small site starts with a great user experience. The elements of making the user experience great—providing context, enabling tasks, and presenting a clear hierarchy—come together as a manageable website that both regular visitors and first-timers can understand and use. Whether your small site is just a single page or 100 pages, its components—things like your logo, navigation, and text—have to be chosen and formatted with the goal of making your site useful for the people who matter: your visitors.

Up to now, I've been describing the ideal small site. That's great if your site is still a doodle on a cocktail napkin. If you already have a website, you may have realized that it falls short of the model explained in this chapter. Maybe it once was a simple, straightforward affair having a few links, some text, some descriptions of your company's products or services, and your logo but has now lost its focus. If you think your website is bloated, it probably is.

Starting with or restoring focus to your website is the key to success when building small, and I'll discuss strategies for identifying and maintaining focus in Chapter 3.

CREATING A FOCUS FOR YOUR SITE

- Learn why focus is critical for a small site.

- Learn how you can create and maintain a good focus for your site.

- Learn important design techniques for creating a single page site.

Why do you have a website, or why are you considering creating one? Because everyone else has one? Wrong. Your website is more than just an online billboard or business card. If all it's doing is validating your business's existence, then it's not doing enough.

Building a website because everyone else has one will result in a site that's indistinguishable from your competition's site. Or worse, you'll end up with a bloated, money-losing site piled up with unnecessary features instead of zeroing in on the ways your website's message can focus on your customers' needs and how you can help them.

In this chapter you'll learn how to create the best type of focus for your site. As you'll learn, the focus is about much more than just how visitors use your site or what they can do on it. A small site's focus—or theme or mission—goes to the heart of your website's reason for being. It helps answer the important question, Why does your site exist at all?

Visitors to your website will ask themselves this question the moment your home page loads, and they will expect a clear answer right away. Find a focus for your site and you'll be on your way to answering this critical question and creating a successful small site.

What Is Focus and Why Is It Important?

Visiting an unfocused website can be as frustrating and disappointing as watching a blurry movie at the multiplex. Your visitors will abandon your site and your business for want of focus. A focused small site makes its purpose immediately clear, and it signals to its visitors that the business behind the site knows its customers' needs.

On a small website focus acts as a filter, giving you a way to determine what's appropriate for your site and what's not appropriate. The content, navigation, tools, and all the other components of a focused site are carefully chosen and tailored to make a meaningful and memorable impact on visitors. What's more, the process of focusing your small site can pay dividends by enhancing your other marketing activities and by giving you better overall clarity in how your business really serves its customers.

Why "Multiple Option" Small Sites Fail

Poorly focused sites confuse their visitors. They make users wonder, "What am I doing here?" The site's purpose becomes difficult or impossible to determine, thanks to the myriad options that mask or inhibit the site's focus: mistargeted advertising that produces little revenue, affiliate programs that benefit the business but distract customers, links to irrelevant "side businesses" or "partners," and hollow content that presents a one-sided view of the business—namely, its own—assuming it gets read at all (see Figure 3.1).

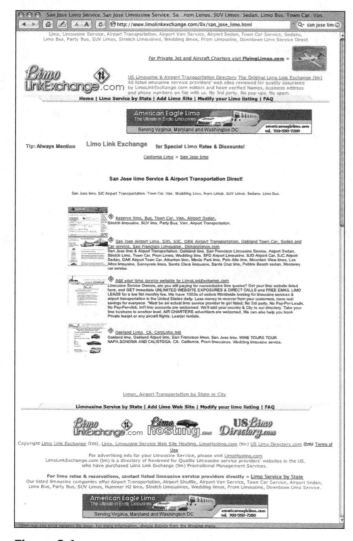

Figure 3.1
Ostensibly a site for a San Jose limousine service, the home page is filled with unfocused busy-ness such as a plug for a flying limo service, promos for a limo link exchange and hosting service, and an ad for a competitor—everything but a link to kitchensink.com.

Choosing a focus for your small site is one area of web publishing where following the big site model can detract from a small site's success. Small sites are not destinations like Amazon.com or Yahoo! Big sites are built for repeat visits, so they can present many focal points, or areas of interest, that users may explore during their visits. The focus of a destination site accumulates over multiple visits, and each person will develop a slightly different perception of what that focus is, especially if they visit the site multiple times.

Many big sites try to be all things to all people. This approach simply does not work for small sites. A small site loses focus—and its visitors' attention—when it gets too big and bloated for the business it represents. Bloated sites offer too many options, which prevent visitors from concentrating on why they came to the site in the first place. For a small site, focus means keeping the message simple and meeting the customer's needs. The goal of focusing your small site is to connect with visitors and start the process that will turn them into customers.

Focus Creates Your Site's First Impression

Consider the typical web surfer who visits your site for the first time. She's impatient, especially if she can't figure out your site's purpose. She wonders, "What's in this for me?" She wants to get in, get what she came for, and move on. Remember that at any moment she's a click or two away from your competition.

Your small site may get only one or two visits from a potential customer—just enough to make or break a customer's decision to do business with you. Given such a brief opportunity to engage a potential customer, a small site must make a positive, lasting first impression on its visitors and distinguish its business from the rest.

Focus Shows You Know Your Customers

Web surfers may be impatient, but they can also be receptive to your site's purpose if they can figure out what it is. A focused site shows that your business understands its customers' problems and speaks their language. Visitors to your website have sought you out, so if you speak their language, they will have confidence that your business can meet their needs. While direct mail clutters their homes, telemarketing calls interrupt dinner, and TV commercials get muted, your customers can use your website at their convenience.

A small site must be focused to take advantage of this, giving visitors the right content at the right time rather than meaningless content and unfocused bloat. A focused site should be organized and presented the way your customers view your business, not the way you yourself view your business. That's easier said that done. To your customers, you are just another plumber, bed and breakfast, or lamp repair shop among the many they are considering.

Don't assume your visitors know your business or are ready to trust you. They don't and they aren't. But they have found your website, so be sure to clearly indicate your business's benefit to them on your home page. Use inviting and situation-specific language so they'll click beyond your home page to find out more about what you offer (see Figure 3.2).

Figure 3.2
The pictures and copy on dispozagage.com describe a specific problem and offer a solution—namely, a specialty product for truckers.

Focus Helps Play Up the Important Details of Your Site

Focus not only helps you decide what to leave off your site, it also emphasizes what is *on* your site. You may have trouble coming to terms with the fact that what you want for your site is not necessarily what your visitors want, or vice versa. Your life story, pictures of your newborn, even the snazzy guest book feature that came with your hosting account—the audience for that kind of stuff just isn't there for a small site.

Focusing your site means aligning yourself with your visitors. What's important to your visitors should be important to you. Something that's not important shouldn't be on your site—unless you want to weight it down with bloat.

For any visitor to your site, the important detail is the one they're currently seeking. But your site cannot provide everything that potential visitors could want. At least not if you want to keep your site small, simple, and successful. Decide what you offer with your site and make it easy to find. Admit to yourself what your site can't offer and offer visitors an alternative, such as a phone number to call, a location to visit, or even links to other sites. Visitors will respect a site (and a business) that knows its limits, and that will make what you *do* offer more appealing.

What Should Be the Focus of My Small Site?

Now that you know the importance of focus for your small site, let's take the next step and look at how you can choose and craft a good focus.

Of course, every business wants one thing above everything else: more business. Ultimately, you may want visits to your website to result in visitors giving you their personal information, buying your products or services, or learning more about or joining your cause.

But using that as the focus of your website won't impress visitors or set your site and your business apart from the rest. With all the get-rich-quick schemes, scams, and spams floating around on the Internet these days, a site that says "What's in it for us?" rather than "How we can help you?" will have a negative effect and turn off many visitors.

To determine the focus for your website, consider the needs and interests of web surfers, which fall into three general categories: information, interaction, and satisfaction. Your customers want to get accurate information quickly, they want to interact with you or other customers, and they want to transact business with you on their schedule. You should try to consider what's unique or advantageous about your business and combine that with the Web's strengths.

Your site's focus lies at the intersection of your business's strengths, your customers' needs, and the Web's effectiveness at providing fast access to information and connecting people. Here are some ideas to start you thinking about ways to focus your website:

- **Create a website that demonstrates your credibility, trust, advantage, product selection, or the distinguishing features of a new product or service.** An informative site will impress visitors with its valuable resources.

- **Create a website that invites visitors to come to your store.** Once you get them to your site, you need to encourage them to request more information, join your mailing list, or make a donation. A site that enables interaction between its visitors and the business helps build an audience of return visitors and new customers.

- **Create a website that affects your visitors' emotions, senses, ego, or desire to get the best deal, be "in the know," or stay one step ahead of the proverbial Joneses.** A site that satisfies its visitors can distinguish your business from its competitors.

Don't lose sleep trying to come up with a ground-breaking focus for your small site. Eureka moments in web publishing are occurring less frequently than they used to—that's an ex-dot-commer's way of saying someone else has already thought of all the good ideas. Just think about how your site can inform, or engage, or satisfy visitors and you'll have a good idea about what your site's focus should be. Before you can think about your home page, your other site pages, or any of the navigation, links, text, or graphics to put on them, you need to settle on your site's purpose. Beware the urge to try to do it all, though. On a small site, lack of focus leads to bloat.

Focus Your Home Page and the Rest of Your Site

In fashioning a focus for your site, you need to look closely at your site in its entirety, but you also need to take a close look at your home page because it's the first thing most visitors to your site will see. We'll start with the home page, and then we'll extend what we learn to other pages on your site.

Applying your focus on your home page in particular might best be summed up by the questions dozens of business owners ask their web designers every week:

- What should I display on my home page?
- How much information can I put on it? How much information is too much?
- How impressive does the home page need to be?
- What is the real purpose of a home page?

Your home page is the first place to start because few visitors to your site are going to make it past your home page. Some will come to your site and quickly leave because your site (business) doesn't offer what they are looking for. Others will leave because they simply get bored quickly. The most important thing to avoid with your home page is giving the wrong impression, thus turning away a visitor who could turn out to be a customer.

For example, if you are in the business of selling inexpensive, custom-made sofas, you don't want to give a visitor to your site the impression that shipping is going to be a big hassle or that your sofas are expensive. Fortunately, there are things within your control that you can do to give visitors the right impression up front and keep them coming back to your site to do more business with you.

A focused home page should introduce your business without overwhelming visitors, give people a reason to stay and explore, and lead visitors to other pages on the site. And every page on your site has to support and reinforce your site's focus—how it serves your customers and how they can make the most of it.

To help you determine a focus for your site, try answering the following questions on your home page, and think about how additional pages can expand on or enhance what's on your home page:

- What one thing do we do best?

- Why did we start this business?

- Why do our customers do business with us?

- How do we making doing business with us easy?

- Who are our main customers and what do they think of us?

- How do we make our customers' lives better or easier or more en-joyable?

- Why are we great at what we do?

- What makes us qualified to create and sell this product?

- What do our products look like?

- How do we know what our customers want?

- What does our business, product, or service make possible?

- What is the defining characteristic of our business?

- What makes our company different from the rest?

Here are some other tips to help you improve the focus of your site:

- **Don't hold back important information.** Often, a website's most relevant information is buried a click or two deep in the site's structure. There's the contact page, the about us page, the products page, the news release page, and so on. When all is said and done, there's nothing left for the home page—the most important page on your site. (I have to believe that this explains the popularity of Flash movies and splash screens in place of a real home page. They fill a void.)

  Don't fall into the trap of thinking that your home page must only provide minimal information. Of course you don't want your home page to become too cluttered, but your first goal needs to be providing enough information to convince your visitors that they have come to the right site.

- **Don't try to provide too much information.** The flip side to not holding back information is creating a site with a home page that appears to promise a lot but subpages that deliver too little. For example, if the home page includes links to subpages for FAQs, services offered, or work samples, don't let people down with underwhelming content when they click to the subpages. If the subpages don't do what the home page says they will, you might be better off with a one-page site, which we'll come back to later in this chapter.

- **Make your home page an easy entry point, but don't let it be an easy exit point.** It's no wonder that for many small sites, the home page is both the most frequent entry *and* most frequent exit point from the site. Your home page needs to draw your visitors in, and thus it becomes the keystone to your website's focus. If it isn't aligned with your customers' interests, most visitors will "say" no more than "hello" and "goodbye." Consider the website for a translation service: It has to quickly inform visitors about the languages it supports, perhaps by using flag icons.

Your concern with additional pages on your site is not so much with losing visitors, but rather with ensuring that they fulfill the "call to action" potential that you established on your home page. For example, a personal trainer has to give site visitors easy access to the application or form for arranging an initial consultation.

- **Make sure your site complements your offline persona.** Don't surprise or confuse visitors to your website with a home page that's inappropriate for your business or industry. A website is a tempting canvas for trying something clever or unexpected, but most of the time attempts at novelty fall flat. Don't distinguish your business with a website out of left field (see Figure 3.3).

- **Make sure the composition of your home page supports its purpose.** Your website's focus will be conveyed through text and images—and not just the subjects of those images or the words you choose to use. The size, placement, and number of graphics on your home page, as well as the size, placement, and length of the text (or lack of text), help announce your site's purpose to visitors (see Figure 3.4).

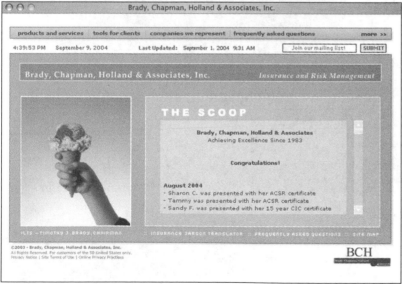

Figure 3.3

A jazz musician's home page (top) hits it right on with a picture of him and his instrument. But can you guess the likely consequence of showing an ice cream cone (above) on the home page for an insurance and risk management firm? That's right—visitor brain freeze.

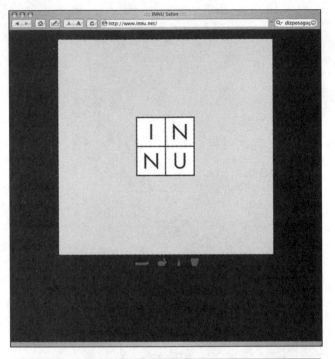

Figure 3.4
You might not want your hair stylist to take tips from
your landscape designer, but this salon site (top) could
learn a thing or two from the landscaping firm's site
(bottom). Innu.net lacks any meaningful text or graphics
(save the logo) to indicate the purpose of the site.
Goodman's site offers work samples and a statement
about its work philosophy on the home page.

- **Consider building a single-page site.** Every page you add to your site has the potential to dilute your focus and create organizational and maintenance challenges that offset the potential benefit of the extra pages. A single-page site offers an alternative approach to getting your business on the Web. With no navigation to solve or links to follow, a one-page site gives visitors the impression that your business is easy to work with.

  One-page sites also have the advantage of being easy to make and keep focused. They do a business card, billboard, or yellow pages ad one better by allowing you to introduce yourself and interact with visitors with a small, simple, and encapsulated presentation. Single-page sites convey a humble, customer-focused way of doing business instead of the aggrandized attitude that screams out from a bloated site.

Examples of Good Website Focus

We've spent a bit of time in this chapter reviewing all of the important concepts that are involved in creating focused websites. Let's finish by considering some small site examples that illustrate the concepts that we have been discussing.

- The owners of a plumbing and heating company might put a few helpful hints or quick tips on their site to demonstrate their expertise and perhaps save customers a phone call. The focus of a site that takes this approach is "We'll help you help yourself." Visitors to your site think, "I feel like this company is already working for me." The Pine Street Plumbing company (**www.pinestatesuddenservice.com**) based in Portland, Maine, is built around customer service, and its website emphasizes this successful business approach and uses it as a calling card. Figure 3.5 shows a customer service FAQ page that the company highlights on its site. In addition to the FAQ page, a helpful newsletter is provided in PDF format (see Figure 3.6) that customers can easily print or download. The newsletter provides a number of money-saving and planning tips. Most of the features provided on the site are designed to emphasize customer service and follow-up. This is a focus that could help any business attract and keep customers.

FINDING YOUR FOCUS

To help you find a better focus for your site, try this simple exercise. Ask yourself this question: My website can help my customers by _____. Note that the question asks about your *website*, not your business. Your answer will vary depending on the nature of your business, but it might be similar to one or more of the following answers:

- My website helps my customers save time.

- My website helps my customers save money.

- My website makes my customers want to work with me.

- My website gives my customers confidence in my products or services.

All of these answers have a common thread: Let you customers' needs guide your focus. Make your customers' life easier by demonstrating how your business can benefit them.

No matter what the size of your business or the budget for your website is, there is a way to focus it that shows you put your customer's needs first and imparts a positive feeling about your business. A focused site helps visitors picture themselves doing business with you.

Figure 3.5
Pine Street's customer service FAQ provides a potential customer with answers to questions like What is a tankless water heater? or What kind of toilet should a customer look for? The information presented might even save some expensive plumbing charges.

- A portrait photographer could use her site to suggest ways that her customers can prepare for their sitting—what to wear, when to arrive, how long it will take, and what the costs are. Visitors to her site would most likely think, "She must be good—she makes it sounds so easy. And she wants me to look good."

- A business that specializes in selling unique products, such as uniquely designed furniture, could emphasize the product's design on the website. Here the focus would be on how unique the products are and how you certainly wouldn't be able to find products like this at a local Target store. A good example of a website that uses this approach is **www.funkysofa.com** (see Figure 3.7). This producer of unique sofas uses its website as a simple showplace to show of its rather "funky" design. A website

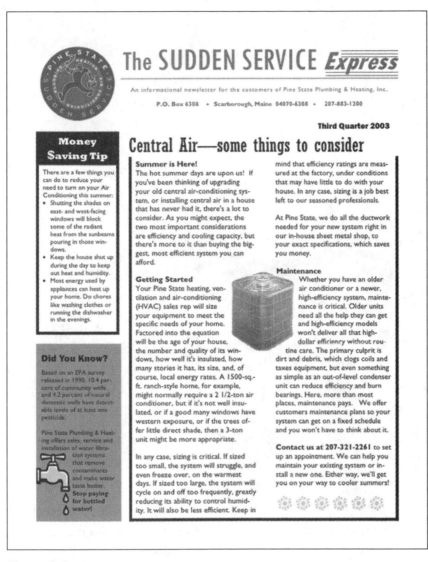

Figure 3.6
In addition to its FAQ, Pine Street's newsletter, *The Sudden Service Express,* is useful vehicle that provides answers to common plumbing problems as well as money-saving tips.

that takes an approach like this should try to stay true to its mission—providing a unique product showcase—and avoid the trappings of sites that try to provide too much clutter and unnecessary information.

Figure 3.7
If you need a sofa or a loveseat that stands out from the pack, funkysofa can help you find it fast. Its unique designs are expertly presented on its site, and you can easily use the site to customize a sofa that you like.

- A lamp repair shop that can build a lamp out of anything might show some common examples of its work. The visitor thinks, "I can picture that kitschy diner-style napkin dispenser as a kitschy lamp."

- A nanny could use her home page to give visitors an overview of how to hire someone in her line of work. As the focus of the site, she is saying, "I've done the research for you—here's what you need to know." The visitor thinks, "She sounds trustworthy; she's not hiding anything — I'll hire her."

- A business that repairs and restores old watches and clocks could suggest ways that people can preserve the timepieces they already have. A landscaper could use his site to list of products he recommends or endorses. The focus of these sites is "We know what we're doing."

- A business that sells a new or unfamiliar product can use testimonials and a targeted feedback form to show that it stands behind its product. The focus of the site is "Our product has helped these people and it can help you too."

Focused sites like the ones presented in these examples create memorable impressions on visitors and helps them understand how the business behind the site can benefit them. An unfocused website leaves visitors questioning its purpose or mission as well as the benefit of working with the business that runs the site.

Designing the Single Page Small Site— The Ultimate Focus

In Chapter 2 we discussed the issues involved in designing small sites. There you learned that a small site can be as simple as a single page or as complex as a multi-page site. Throughout this book I'll be showing examples of different types of sites to illustrate different concepts, such as navigation techniques, methods for displaying content, and so on. Many of the examples I'll provide will be from sites that contain multiple pages simply because it is easier to use such sites to show you the concepts that I need to present.

As we learned earlier, a single page site needs to really function like an ad (think Yellow Pages) that provides some type of call to action. A single page site is also a more appropriate vehicle for a small business like a B&B, restaurant, tour guide operator, independent doctor, attorney, or dentist, real estate agent, consultant, and so on. Businesses that also provide highly targeted products and services can also benefit from having a single page site.

Designing a single page site might seem like an easy process, but once you try it you'll soon see that it is more complicated. Doing this takes a certain type of mindset that might at first seem counterintuitive, especially if you are used to working with a medium like the Web where space seems almost infinite. For example, if you were designing a house you could easily see the physical space that you have to work with. Or if you were an author writing a book you could readily see that your book could only contain a fixed number of pages. The Web, on the other hand, has hidden boundaries that almost give the designer the impression that a site can be as big as it wants to.

The mindset you need to adopt for creating a single page site reminds me of something I once read about the difference between painting and photography. A painter starts with a blank canvas and considers his job to be one of adding elements to create a composition. A photographer, on the other hand, starts with a full scene and its his job to remove as much as he can to create an artistic impression. As a designer of a single page site, you need to think like a photographer, start with a list of all of the elements that you think are important for your single page site, and then remove as much as you can. What you are left with then is the real essentials of what makes your site communicate the best to your audience.

In this section I'll walk you through the process of designing a single page site. But before we examine the types of features that should be included in a single page site, let's look at a an example of successful single page site.

The single page site shown in Figure 3.8 is for a lodging camp and guide service in Maine called Buck's Crossing. This site provides an excellent balance of photos and text to communicate the services that the business provides. I don't know about you but I just really love the company's marketing message: "The Way Life Should Be." When I read this message and view the photos I just want to pick up the phone and call 207-277-3183 and make my reservation. There's no question in my mind about what the business has to offer me.

From looking at the examples just presented, one thought you might have is that there isn't a fixed set of features that must be provided on every small site. Of course, there are some common elements that should always be presented. To help step you through the design process, let's look at both the common elements all sites should have and the more unique elements that can be provided. I'll also give you some suggestions about features you should definitely avoid

Common Elements for Single Page Sites

Every single page site simply needs to answer a few basic questions such as what is the business' name?; what type of business is represented?; and how is the business contacted? The common elements that should be included are:

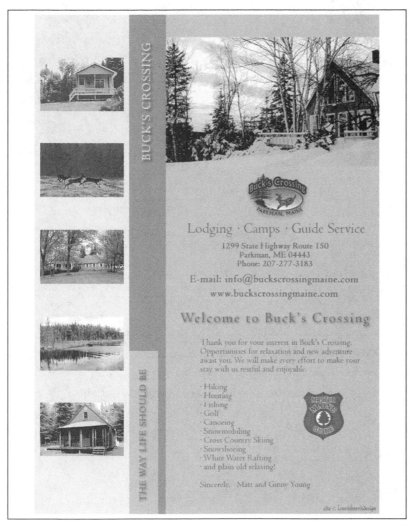

Figure 3.8
Buck's Crossing at **http://buckscrossingmaine.com/** uses the
single page format well to present its unique offerings.

- Company name

- Business logo (which generally should be placed in the upper-left
  corner, or in the top portion of the home page)

- Contact information

- Clear and concise description of the product or service that you
  provide

- A photo if appropriate to convey an important message about your
  company

- A simple marketing message

- Some type of call to action

In addition, all of the graphics should be optimized to ensure that the load time is as fast as possible. The most critical information for your site should be placed in the first screen if all of your information does not fit in one screen and the user needs to scroll down. Typically, you should allocate the first 400 to 600 vertical pixels for your most critical information.

In laying out your site, try to be as consistent as you possibly can. Keep the single page simple by using a basic color scheme, text size, font size, and format. Varying these attributes can make your single page look unprofessional, inconsistent and hard to read. Try to reorient vertical or highly stylized display copy in a way that's horizontal and more readable (monitors are hard to turn 90 degrees!) Use no more than, say, three different color and fonts on your single page. Keep clutter to a minimum.

Elements that Depend on Your Situation (Unique Ones)

Because no single type of business is exactly like another type of business, it's impossible to create a full list of elements that all single page sites must have. Here I've provided a list of elements that you can pick from to add to the list of common elements to support your type of business. For example, if your business is some type of retail store, you should include your hours of operation.

- Your hours of operation
- Testimonials
- Special information about areas of specialization
- Information on special offers
- Basic information on shipping/customer service
- Links to a site for ordering products
- Endorsements or awards, where appropriate
- Links to obtain more information about your company, products, or services

Elements that You Shouldn't Bother to Present

To keep your site down to a single page, there is a lot of information that you need to leave out:

- *Detailed descriptions of your products or services.* You simply won't have the space for this so don't even try.

- *Any type of Flash animation, complex graphics, or audio.* Real estate is at a premium at a single page site so keep off the clutter. Besides, a visitor to a single page site doesn't have the time to bother with stuff like this.

- *Shopping cart.* This is a feature for bigger sites. If you have a small business and you want to use a single page site to promote your business, let the telephone or fax be your ordering system of choice.

- *Navigation features.* If your site is a single page, the viewer can simply scroll to find information they need. Try to keep the number of links that you have on your page down to a minimum.

- *Contact Us form.* Just providing an email address is all you need. A Contact Us form is nice for larger sites but it will likely just be a source of clutter for a single page site.

Summary

Finding and maintaining a focus for your website is the crucial first step in building a successful small site. The direction you take with the rest of your site—the navigation, content, and functionality components—follows directly from the site's focus. A good focus will help distinguish your site from those of your competitors and quickly answers the question most first-time visitor ask: Why does this site exist?

Focus creates your site's first impression. Because a focused website shows that your business knows and respects your customers, it can be the deciding factor in a visitor's decision to do business with you. In Chapter 4, we'll explore how to implement your focus with the right design format and navigation choices.

USE THE RIGHT DESIGN AND NAVIGATION FORMAT
4

- Learn how to select a design approach that works for your website by considering the pros and cons of a palette of small site designs.

- Learn how you can use images and graphics to better brand your small site.

- Learn which navigation and design techniques will make your site really usable.

I f you are planning a new website or thinking about redesigning your existing site, you have no doubt seen—and probably bookmarked—some snazzy-looking websites to inspire yourself or your web designer. In many ways, designing a website—and having the ability to combine color, animation, photography, and interesting text treatments—is a prime opportunity to be creative. A website is an empty canvas, a blank slate.

But your favorite design may not be compatible with keeping your site small and successful. Design should complement your website's focus or purpose. In the same way that focus filters what should and shouldn't go on your site, an appropriate design disciplines your site development.

In this chapter, we'll look at the role of design in a website and how a site's design influences how the site comes across to its visitors. We'll also look at design's close cousin—navigation—to see how the two are related to the effectiveness of your site.

The Role of Design

If you get stuck in room with a group of web designers you'll hear a lot of talk about page load times, HTML and XML, color and page sizes, animated graphics, and the latest design gizmos. Designers love to talk about the tools they use and the latest design trends. But hidden in all of this conversation are the real issues that you should pay attention to such as how a certain type of design is used to improve usability or create a strong sense of trust between a website and a visitor. You also might hear discussions about how different types of fonts are used to improve readability or how page links are used to help break up text into smaller, more easily readable sections. This is the "language" of design that you should always be on the lookout for.

The design of your website plays a part in delivering the unspoken or unwritten message of your business. A good design helps keep your website interesting, structured, and usable—and, by association, casts your business in a favorable light.

A Good Visual Design Engages Your Visitors

The Web's strength as a visual medium is unquestioned. Often, a site is as much about what it looks like as what it says or does. Some sites exist for no other reason than to push the envelope of what's possible in web design.

Your small site will not be one of those sites. But, your site should exhibit some aesthetic sensibility. As several design experts and professional aestheticians have asserted, there is no undesigned object. In the world of commercial products at least, design pervades everything from cell phone face plates to toilet brushes. Surrounded by "designed objects" at every turn in their everyday life, visitors to your site will likewise expect your website to have a "design."

Design in this sense does not imply avant-garde or cutting edge, but rather it means produced with a purpose. A designed site employs visual discipline to support the site's mission and connect with its visitors.

Design Keeps Everything in Its Right Place

As focus does, design helps determine if something—an advertisement, logo, image, text block or other graphical element—is appropriate for the site. Not "appropriate" in terms of its content, but appropriate in how its size, color, and composition affect the site's design for better or worse.

In a well-designed site, areas of pages with different functions are separate and consistent across all the pages. A site's design should clearly delineate areas of a site by function. For a small site, that primarily means designing a site with distinct areas for your logo or brand, navigation buttons and links (which we'll come back to later in this chapter), content, and a page footer, which might hold a copyright notice, page modification date, email link to the webmaster, and other short, site usage information. Larger sites might also designate web page real estate for other purposes, such as tools (search, shopping, or account management) and marketing, advertising, or promotional messages.

The creators of cluttered sites have "bent the rules" too many times, resulting in a visual mishmash that confuses visitors. As the proverb goes, a room full of people may refuse to acknowledge the elephant in their midst. But a site that has grown bloated without regard for an overarching design principle will be noticeable to all who see it.

Design Orients Visitors

As you saw in Chapter 2 when I discussed the key components of the user experience, people can easily become disoriented on the Web. A well-designed site is an antidote to the problem.

Bloated sites often have a disturbing "designed on the fly" look to them. Like something shiny in the monkey cage, a new website feature captivates the bloated site builder and diverts attention from the rest of the site. On a small site, the latest-and-greatest look is avoided so that a design that's simple and customer focused can be maintained.

A well-conceived and consistent design helps draw attention to what has changed as the visitor moves from page to page. Ideally, what changes is the most important part of the page, the stuff your customer is interested in. The rest of the site recedes to the periphery, getting attention from the visitor only when necessary. By abandoning consistent design from page to page, visitors to a bloated site are forced to concentrate on how the site is organized rather than on how the site and the business can benefit them.

Components of Site Format/Design Approach

Each component of a website's design factors into how the site is received by visitors, so let's look at some specific components of a site's design and the role they play.

Color Scheme: Background Colors and Images

The background on your web pages serves as your site design's foundation. Together and separately, the background color and background image you use go a long way toward determining how the site is perceived by visitors. You might be tempted to use a full-screen background image to embellish your site, thinking it will make your site look bigger, better, and more professional than it is. Resist the urge. You likely don't need to display a full-screen image to convey the important information

you need to present. A large image will be slow to load and will probably turn off your customers.

In general, background images, whether they are whole images or
tiled patterns, tend to detract from a site's design. Computer monitor
resolutions are much lower than the resolution of text printed with ink
on paper, so web page legibility is already a challenge. Images of varying tone and contrast that lurk behind the text of every page
compound the problem and frustrate visitors, especially older users
and those with less-than-perfect eyesight. Like "click here" or blinking
text, background images can be a telltale sign of bloat.

That said, background images can be used effectively in areas of your
web pages where they won't appear underneath text. In small doses,
background images can divide sections in your design or add an artistic flair to the edge of your pages. (See Figures 4.1, 4.2, and 4.3 for

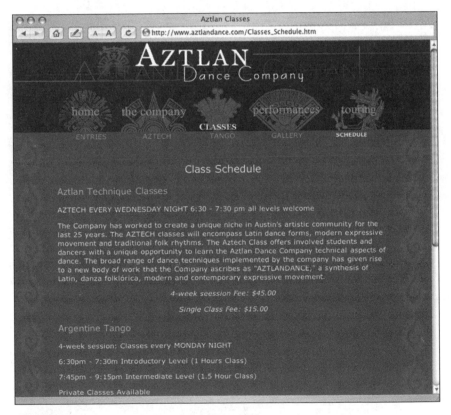

Figure 4.1
A dance company website makes effective use of background colors and
images. The site evokes the richness of experiencing a performance.

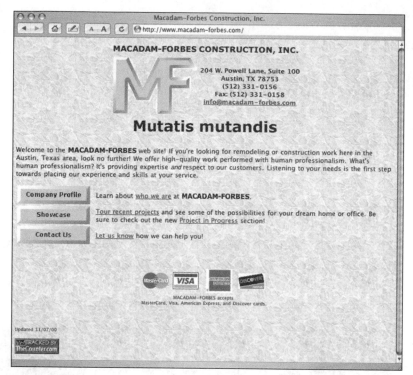

Figure 4.2
The use of a textured background for a construction company
website detracts from the site's design.

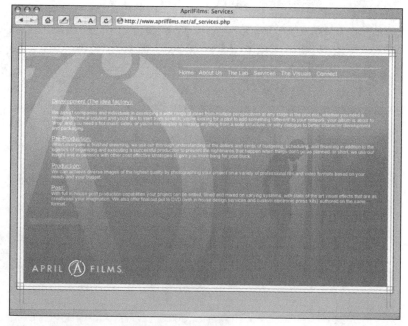

Figure 4.3
A stylized full-screen background image on this visual production
company website evokes the high quality of their work but makes
the small website copy really hard to read.

examples of backgrounds and background images used effectively and not so effectively.)

Background colors, on the other hand, have a much better reputation. In fact, they can be an integral part of a site's color scheme and overall design—small or large.

Though far from being a black-and-white issue, the spectrum of impressions generated by background colors runs roughly from luxury, mystery, entertainment, or a glimpse of an experience (with black or dark colors) to familiarity, necessity, or utility of informational sites (with white or lighter colors). Choose your background color wisely because it conveys a lot about your site's focus, mission, and purpose (see Figures 4.4, 4.5, 4.6, and 4.7 for examples. Because this book was printed in black and white, I strongly suggest that you take a moment to look these pages up on the web so that you can view the background colors.)

Figure 4.4
Mr. Broadway's black background says "show biz!"

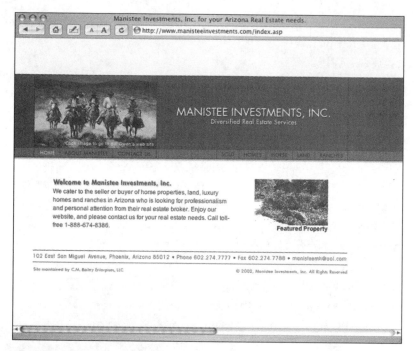

Figure 4.5
Earth tones on the site of an Arizona real estate firm evoke images of the open range.

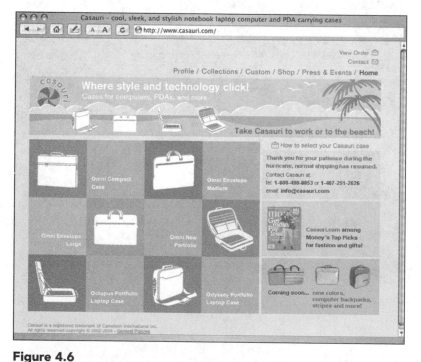

Figure 4.6
Pastel green on an e-commerce site that sells computer cases makes the site "fun."

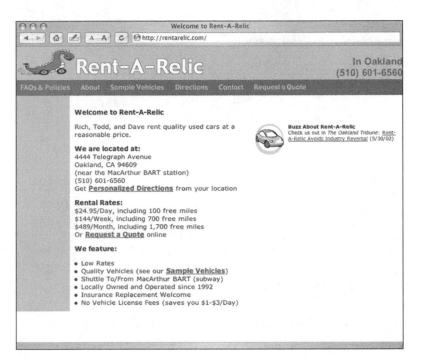

Figure 4.7
A white background on this site for an Oakland-based car rental firm keeps visitors focused on getting the information they came for.

Page Grid and Navigation Zones

Most newspapers or magazines you see on your local newsstand have a professional look because they follow a well-defined grid from page to page and from issue to issue. A grid, or template, dictates where structural elements like page numbers go and establishes rules for things like column width and image size that dictate how pages should look.

You can achieve a similar professional look with your web pages by following a template or grid and basing all of your pages on it. A website grid divides your pages into areas for navigation, content, and other uses, such as marketing or advertising messages, administrative notices, or e-commerce tools (see Figure 4.8). Having a grid like this can really help ensure that you follow a consistent design layout for your site. If you take the time to look at some sites that have a consistent design, you'll likely find that they are based on a consistent design grid. By looking at different sites that you like, you'll be better able to produce a design grid of your own.

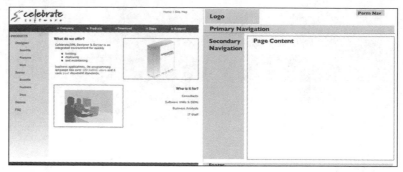

Figure 4.8
A page grid or template, like this one (right) for a small software company website (left), enforces design consistency on all the pages of your site.

A grid is one of the strongest methods for enforcing consistency and avoiding clutter on your site. Consistency, in turn, evokes reliability, integrity, and trustworthiness. If you can't find a place in your grid for something you want to add, then it probably doesn't belong there.

Small sites tend to be updated infrequently. And when the time comes to add a new page, it's usually enhanced with a "need it done yesterday" urgency. Basing your web pages on a predetermined template prevents the bloat-inducing mutations that occur when you design as you go.

You may want or need to deviate from your grid in some cases. For example, you may want to offer site-search results hosted on a third-party site or create a stripped-down special offer response page. A well-designed site should be flexible enough to accommodate this. Another common way the page grid is altered on many sites is by creating a home page that references the design of the rest of the site while not strictly adhering to it (see Figure 4.9).

Photography and Illustrations

Images can enhance your site with color and human interest and give it impact that text cannot. Visitors with no time to read your site may judge it on the size, placement, choice of images and—above all—the time it takes the images to load. The load time is especially important for small sites.

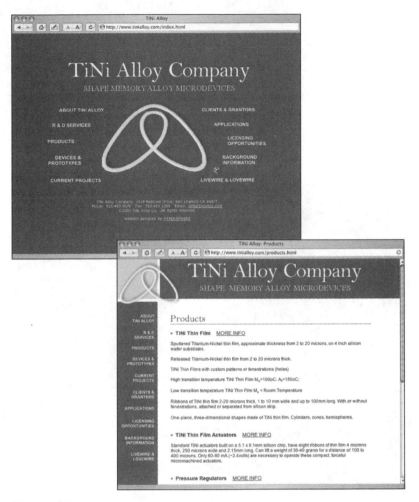

Figure 4.9
The TiNi Alloy Company home page shares a logo and typeface
with the rest of the site's pages, but not their "inverted L" layout.

Gone are the days of home pages dominated by ponderous image
maps—the full-screen representational graphics implanted with links
to the rest of the site. In their place are sites overloaded with graphics,
but the effect is the same—at least in terms of page-load time. If the
"weight" of a page on your site—the cumulative file size of the images
and HTML—exceeds about 40 or 50 kilobytes, the page will load too
slowly and the impact of your well-chosen graphics will be lost.

There are two ways to put pages on a diet. The first way is to use image
editing software like Photoshop or Fireworks to optimize the graphics to
the smallest reasonable file size as measured in bytes or kilobytes. When
you're deciding how far to go when optimizing, remember that users
may not notice a loss of fidelity if the page loads quickly.

Another way to trim down your pages is to use fewer images more effectively or create composite images to present a theme or idea of many separate images. Remember the Small Site mantra: Less is more.

Finally, a warning about using stock photography: With so many sources of free photography available of the Web, there are some very familiar images and themes floating around out there (see Figure 4.10).

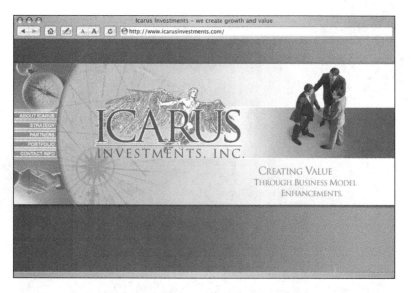

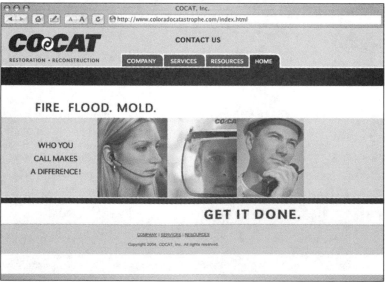

Figure 4.10
Common themes of website stock photography include businessmen shaking hands and operators standing by—hey, is that Uma Thurman? I don't know about you, but I see way to many sites using these clip-art clichés.

Typefaces

Typefaces and fonts play an important role in your site's design by establishing hierarchy on pages. You want to use a large font for headlines and subheads, a medium-sized font for the main text on your pages, and a small font for things like your page footer, credits, and copyright notice.

But don't mistake hierarchy for variety. As with the well-known rule of print design, the fewer font families you use in your website design, the better. In fact, using one or two families—not counting the one you use in your logo—is sufficient.

Print guidelines often recommend serif typefaces—the ones with little embellished curves on their ends—for body copy, but the bulk of your website copy should be set in a sans-serif typeface. The low resolution of computer monitors renders serif fonts more poorly than sans-serif faces. Of the many sans-serif choices, an online legibility study a few years back deemed Verdana the most readable—though fonts like Helvetica, Arial, Tahoma, and Trebuchet MS are worthy alternatives (see Figure 4.11).

The quick brown fox jumped over the lazy dogs - Verdana.

The quick brown fox jumped over the lazy dogs - Arial.

The quick brown fox jumped over the lazy dogs - Helvetica.

The quick brown fox jumped over the lazy dogs - Trebuchet MS.

The quick brown fox jumped over the lazy dogs - Tahoma.

Figure 4.11
Examples of some of the most readable typefaces for web pages.
From the top: Verdana, Arial, Helvetica, Trebuchet MS, and Tahoma.

USE IMAGES AND GRAPHICS THAT HELP BRAND YOUR SITE

If you haven't given your business's brand any thought lately, then you may not have been paying enough attention. These days, it seems, everything from a century-old museum to a middle manager contemplating a career change needs to have a "brand." Long gone are the days when a brand was simply a scar on the hindquarters of a 1300-pound steer (see Figure 4.12). Today brands take the form of ubiquitous logos and acronyms with buzzword ambitions, among other things.

Beneath the hype, however, lies the reality that a good brand identifies a successful business. But slapping a swoosh or a catchphrase on your website does not a brand make. Branding is about uniting the tangible components of your business, like your logo or tagline, with intangible attributes, such as how your business fulfills its promise to its customers.

For a small business with limited resources, branding may seem like the province of big, multinational companies. So look at it this way: A brand is simply something

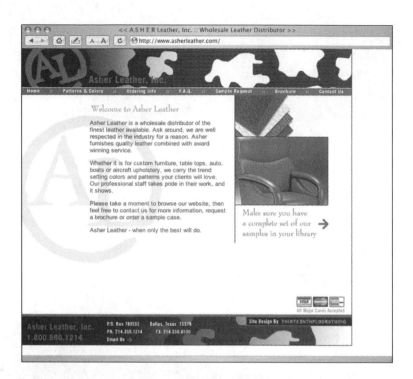

Figure 4.12
A handful of subtle enhancements make this leather furniture store's website memorable: the logo (a real brand, no less) reused as a ghosted backdrop behind the main content area, the Holstein header image, the logo typeface reused for graphical subheads, and the graphic cowhide-to-sofa pattern (above).

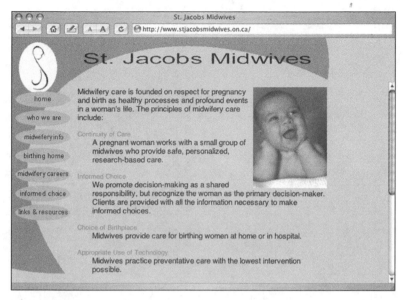

Figure 4.13
The bulging shape divides content from navigation on a midwives practice website.

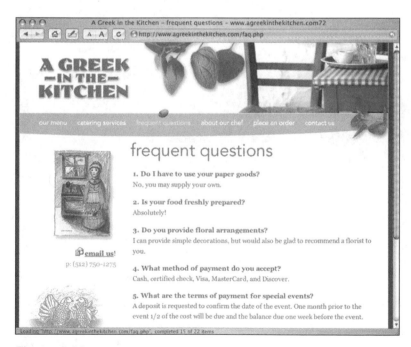

Figure 4.14
A catering service specializing in Greek cuisine tops its navigation links with an olive to indicate the section of the site the visitor is looking at.

that your customers and potential customers can use to identify and remember your business as the one that can solve their problem. It should reinforce why your customers do business with you or, better yet, why your customers shouldn't even think about doing business with your competitors.

While a small business brand can't be built overnight, here are a few graphical techniques to make your small site stand out from the rest:

- Extend motifs or familiar imagery from your logo to subheads, icons, or the overall layout of your site (see Figures 4.13 through 4.16).

- Use images of people—from stock photos, if necessary—to reinforce your customer focus (see Figure 4.17).

- Use logos or endorsements to emphasize your expertise (see Figure 4.18).

Figure 4.15
A subtle drop shadow frames a work-sample slide show and portrays the architectural photographer who took them as suitable for hiring.

Figure 4.16
Price-tag-shaped buttons mark the navigation of the children's clothing purveyor.

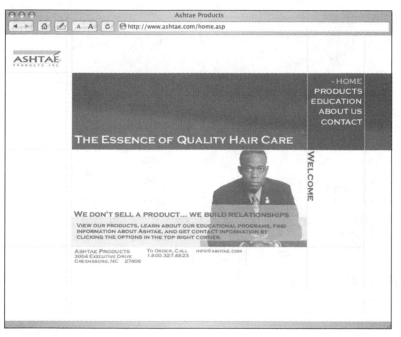

Figure 4.17
A human face can personalize your site and help you connect with
visitors.

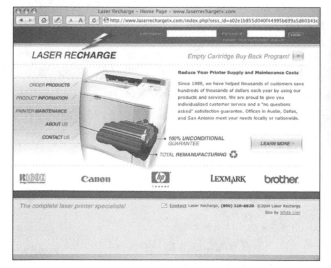
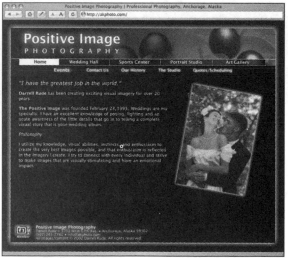

Figure 4.18
Logos of the products you service (top) or the professional organizations to which you belong (bottom,
lower left) can distinguish your site—and your business—from the rest.

Bear in mind, however, that you have limited control over the typefaces used to render your page in a user's browser. Their browser may not have your preferred font installed, or they may have configured their browser to override the fonts and styles of every web page, substituting their favorite font instead.

Components of Navigation

The navigation style of your site is closely related to your site's overall design. You want your navigation to fit with your page grid, stick to your color scheme, and be presented in complementary and readable fonts. But most of all, your navigation should help visitors get to the information they want from your site simply and quickly.

Navigation Types and Position

Whether you use images or plain text, the navigation links that guide visitors come in four varieties —primary, secondary, permanent, and functional—though you may see all four only on a large site like Amazon.com. A single-page site won't have any navigation (since there aren't any other pages to link to) and a small site might only have a few main links and a permanent "Contact Us" link at the bottom of every page.

The primary navigation should be the most prominent kind of navigation in your design. It identifies the six to eight main sections of your site, even if a section is just one page. The secondary navigation differs from section to section and provides links to supplemental pages below the main page of a primary link. If you have a lot of secondary navigation, your site may not be a "small site." Large sites may even have tertiary (or third-level) and fourth-level navigation.

On a small site, some of your main site areas (primary navigation links) might have subpages that require secondary links for navigation and some that don't. Don't feel compelled to create additional secondary pages for sections that don't need them just because other sections have them.

Also, avoid the tendency to make every page on your site a primary navigation link. For example, if you have a "Contact Us" link, you probably don't need one that says "Map & Directions." Those navigation links can go on the contact page. Likewise, you can make an "About Us" or "News" page home to links to your latest news releases, as well as information about your intern program or recent awards you've won, rather than making each one a primary link of its own.

The permanent navigation contains small and easy-to-get-to links that don't fit into the primary structure of the site but need to be on every page—things like "Site Map," "Contact Us," and the like. The functional navigation includes links for special sections or actions on your site, such as search results or a shopping cart. Your small site may not have any functional navigation.

Navigation Position and Enhancers

Where you place your site's navigation is less important than keeping it in the same place throughout your site. Basing your site design on a grid or template ensures that your navigation maintains a consistent location.

The top of the page is the safest and most common place for primary navigation. Permanent navigation might sit above it or perhaps at the bottom of the page with your copyright notice.

Many sites use the classic "inverted L" design, so-called for the top bar and left-hand sidebar placement of primary and secondary navigation. The scheme is common among large sites and offers small sites with big plans room to grow.

Many small sites without the need for extensive secondary navigation follow the "inverted L" format but leave one leg of the "L" empty of navigational elements since it does show the company name (see Figure 4.19). Top navigation bars provide quick access to the main sections of your site. Tabs are a popular variation on the top navigation

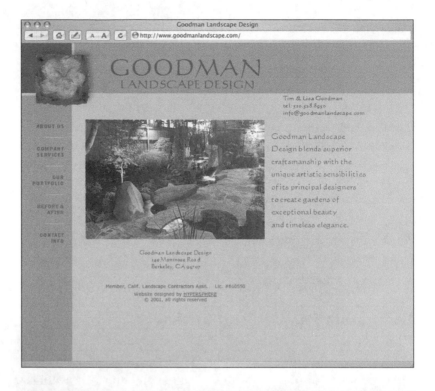

Figure 4.19
Two small sites that use the "inverted L" grid, but leave one leg empty of navigation: A landscaping company site and the site of a therapeutic products company.

bar found on many small sites (see Figure 4.20). Navigation bars, while limited by the horizontal width of the screen, can be expanded with JavaScript- or Java-based drop-down menus for secondary navigation, if necessary. Sidebar placement of primary navigation offers arguably more room, especially for sites with longer navigation phrases.

Figure 4.20
Sites for a temp agency and children's book publisher (top and bottom) both offer a small and effective number of tabs for navigation.

Other ways to enhance your site's navigation include breadcrumb links and icons. Breadcrumb links show a link-based path through the site's structure to the current page. They give visitors a way to jump one or more levels up in the site's structure. Breadcrumbs are most effective in deep sites with lots of sub- and sub-subpages.

Icons are commonly used—and commonly misused—as enhancements to a site's navigation. Notoriously cryptic and open to interpretation (see Figure 4.21), icons are best used sparingly for familiar website actions, such as an envelope icon for a contact form or

Figure 4.21
Don't leave visitors guessing what the icons (top right) on your site mean, like this otherwise attractive site for a Virginia coffeehouse does. Visitors must place their mouse pointer on an icon to get an equally cryptic label.

shopping cart for reviewing order contents. Icons are always themselves enhanced by text labels that explain the resulting action (see Figure 4.22).

Figure 4.22
The Whitman Homes website uses several navigation strategies effectively: icons supported by text labels for the permanent/functional navigation, a top bar for the primary navigation with drop-down menus for the secondary navigation, and breadcrumb links on every page.

Figure 4.23
Top and left aren't the only place to put your primary navigation. Nontraditional navigation placement—wrapped along the side of the mannequin (top) or in a horizontal bar across the middle of the home page (bottom)—makes a positive impact. These sites provide good examples of taking a nontraditional approach but making the navigation really clear to the visitor.

Nontraditional Navigation

I have been showing and emphasizing navigation methods that involve placing the main navigation components on the top and left of web pages. If you are both careful and creative, you can vary this and still create pages that are easy to navigate (see Figure 4.23). In taking an approach like this, the important thing to keep in mind is that you must provide the visitors to your site with the necessary visual clues so that they can quickly and easily see where the navigation features are located. If a visitor has to hunt for a while to find a navigation element on your site, you can be certain that your design isn't working as well as it should be.

I once went to New York City for a business meeting. I arrived at a big impressive building on Fifth Avenue well before the meeting was to start, walked through the lobby and over to the elevator, and then spent five minutes trying to find the button for the elevator. The button was cleverly designed into the artwork on the wall, and if you didn't know exactly where to look, you could easily get frustrated with this important navigation element!

As crazy as this story sounds, this kind of thing happens all the time on the web. Just think about all of the websites that you have visited where you have to hunt for the navigation features. Think about all of the sites that you use that provide standard navigation features in unusual ways. My impression is that the web designers think that they are being really creative but the only thing they are doing is creating an unpleasant experience for the visitor to the site. People who visit your website simply don't have the time to waste learning how to use nontraditional navigation features. They likely will give up and go visit another site. If you work really hard to make a great site, the last thing you want to do is chase a potential customer away because your navigation features are too confusing. As an example, take a look at the site featured in Figure 4.24. The navigation feature is so confusing because it requires the user to move the mouse around just to find a button to click on. When I was younger I used to play hide and seek a lot. It was a fun game. But as an adult the last thing I want to do is play hide and seek on the web!

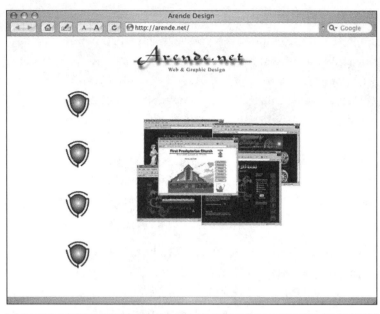

Figure 4.24
This site (top) requires users to pass their mouse over the icons on the left (top) in order to reveal the navigation choices (bottom).

Summary

In this chapter, you learned about the various design and navigation formats you might choose for your site. We looked at how the right design can make your site engaging and usable for the people who visit it. You also learned tips and techniques associated with individual design and navigation components and how they can be arranged in a grid or template that ensures consistency on your site from page to page.

Even with all the rules and guidelines to follow, your website design can and should be a unique expression of your business. Starting with a design grid or template to guide the choice and placement of navigation, color, text, and images will help you stick to a plan and give visitors an appealing impression of your business. With a positive first impression secured in the minds of your site's visitors, you can offer them what they came looking for—content and functionality, which we will discuss in Chapter 5.

TIPS AND TECHNIQUES FOR CONTENT AND FUNCTIONALITY THAT USERS LOVE

5

- Learn to zero in on the information and tasks that your customers will find most informative and useful.

- Learn how to format the text, graphics, and photos on your small site to maximize their impact.

- Learn how to use space wisely when you are building small.

Asmall site's content and functionality should complement each other. The content and functionality on a small site go hand in hand. To be effective, the functionality should lead people to the content they're seeking. They can make your site frustrating and unintelligible when they are out of balance or when one is created and used without the other in mind.

Content is the catchall term for the myriad ways your site can present information: the words and images that fill the main section of your site, downloadable documents, and multimedia content such as video, audio, and animations. Functionality helps visitors to your site find, format, or interact with the content of your site through tools such as search engines, pop-up windows, printable pages, links, and forms.

In this chapter, you'll learn how to create a symbiotic relationship between content and functionality on your website. You'll see how to format the text, photos, and other graphics to maximize their impact on site visitors and how to use links, menus, and even site search to get people to the content they're seeking. You'll also learn how small details like page titles, link titles, meta tags for search engines, alt tags for images, and sample input for your web forms—collectively called *microcontent*—go a long way toward making sure that your site provides the right content to your visitors when they want it.

The Devil Is in the Microcontent

Great small sites start with well-written and useful microcontent. *Microcontent* is the name web usability experts have given to the text that guides people to the content and explains the functionality on a site: page titles, page headlines, link text, navigation phrases, meta tags, image alt tags, sample form input, and form error messages.

Email subject lines, though not a standard part of website content, are a good example of microcontent. If you have ever been annoyed by an email from a friend or colleague with a generic subject line like "hello" or "website"—or worse, a blank subject line—then you know the frustration of poor or missing microcontent and the benefit of microcontent that's useful and to the point.

On your website, microcontent keeps your visitors from getting frustrated and from feeling like they're going around in circles. It also will reduce the number of emails and calls you get from customers asking you to explain your website—assuming they care enough to even ask instead of moving to someone else's site.

Remember that no matter how much effort you put into creating a "path" through your site that you expect visitors to follow, your site will not be viewed or used linearly. Your web pages will be linked from search results pages (Google's or your own search engine) and will be viewed out of context. Industry-specific directories and even people you've never met may "deep link" to pages on your site without regard for the preferred route you laid out for them from your home page.

Let's dig a little deeper and explore some of the components of a website, such as page titles, linked text, and so on, that are part of a successful site's microcontent.

Make Your Page Titles and Headlines More Readable

Page titles (the text in the title bar of the browser window) and page headlines help explain the difference between two pages when seen in a list of links or even in the history menu of the browser. For example, the titles "Acme Corp. Home Page" and "Product List - Acme Corp." are much better choices for two different pages than "Acme Corp." for both pages. Even worse would be to use the all too common default title like "Designed with Adobe GoLive 4.0."

Page titles and headlines should be about four to six words long, and the first word or two should be the most important, unique, or action-oriented or convey the most information. In the previous example, "Product List - Acme Corp" wins out over "Acme Corp – Product List" for just that reason.

Choose a style and naming convention for your page titles and headlines—and stick to it. Consistency in this area will be noticed, and that's a good thing. Variations in your style will make your site look inconsistent and your business unreliable or lacking in attention to detail.

You can separate the site name from the page name in the page title with any character you want—hyphens, colons, a vertical bar, or something else—but use the same one every time. For headlines, you may choose either headline style, where only the first word is capitalized (as well as proper nouns and acronyms), or title style, where all words are capitalized. But, by *all means,* avoid ALL CAPS because every readability study since shortly after Gutenberg has shown ALL CAPS text to be hard to read.

Use action words and write in active voice whenever possible. For example, "We received your comment" makes a better headline on an acknowledgement page than "Your comment has been received." Also, use caution when being clever or cute: plain language works best. Even if you really think you know your customers or audience, your inside joke may be lost on many of them and especially the first-time visitors to your site. Figure 5.1 shows an example of a web page that uses a page title effectively and one that doesn't.

From a search-engine-ranking and click-through perspective, the page title is one of the most important tags on your website, if not *the* most important. Visitors who find out about and visit your site from search engine results are a more focused breed of web surfer. They're also more skeptical and less patient than other visitors to your site. Your site will be judged by its page titles in the same way that a book will be judged by its cover.

Your page titles have to be strong enough to stand on their own because they will appear out of context in a page of search results. Like your entry in the yellow pages, page titles help to classify your site when it's listed among other similar sites in search results. When worded correctly for the type of visitor you are seeking, page titles can boost your click-through from Google and other search engines even if you're not at the top of the rankings. In addition to or in place of a short descriptive phrase about your business, you might consider naming your key benefit, identifying a free offer, or even posing an intriguing question in your page titles.

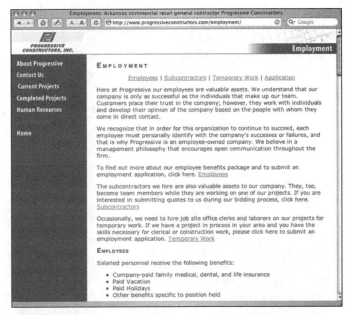

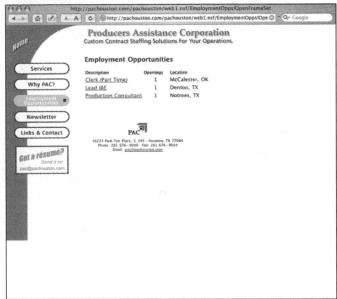

Figure 5.1
The employment pages of two small company websites:
The page title in the browser window bar (top) provides a
meaningful description of the page's contents. On the
PAC Houston website (bottom), the page title isn't even
offered in English.

Balance Visual Cues with Content Detail

The need for good microcontent doesn't end at the top level of the page. Small content details based in microcontent can provide visual cues for your site visitors that make a big difference.

The text you choose to highlight as links, as well as image alt tags and page meta tags, add to the collective usefulness of your site. Links and error messages help visitors quickly identify what they're looking at and what they can do with it. Other types of microcontent operate behind the scenes, hidden from view until needed.

Meta tags and alt tags are embedded in the HTML code of your web pages, giving guidance or additional information to visitors as they move through your site. While meta tags have been in a state of per-petual decline in their importance to search engine rankings, they are important nonetheless for giving searchers a synopsis of the page when seen in a list of search results. You may wish to write one meta tag de-scription for all the pages on your site and then modify or replace it entirely on pages that warrant special treatment.

Alt (alternative text) and title tags can be used to describe the subject of an image or the action that results from clicking a link. For ex-ample, setting headlines and subheads as graphics can be an effective way to extend your site's visual motif, but the content of the image can't be easily indexed and may be missed altogether if a sluggish connection to your website prevents it from loading. Adding text to the image alt tag that matches the graphical headline text ensures that something meaningful will load in the browser in that spot even if the image does not (see Figure 5.2).

And whatever you do, don't set large blocks of text such as your con-tact information, directions to your business, or product instructions as a graphic. In addition to being costly and time-consuming to update, text set as a graphic can't be copied to an email or PDA for future reference.

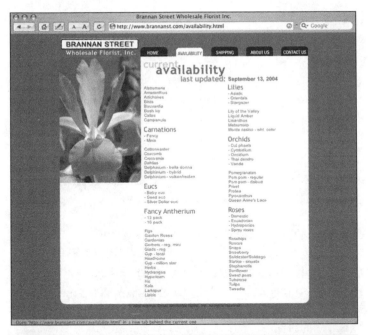

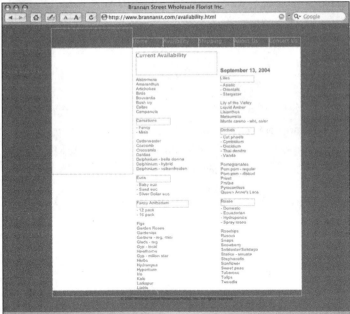

Figure 5.2
A florist's website uses graphics to display the headline and subheads on its product availability page (top). If the graphics don't load, text-based alt tags take their place (bottom).

Link Text and Link Actions

I've already offered my rant (and that of others) against the practice of using the generic and unimaginative "Click here" as link text, so I won't repeat it here. (Except to say that it's a horrible idea and if you don't believe me, go back to Chapter 1.) Links should tell people exactly what they will get when they click. It is also a good idea not to highlight words in text that could be confused as links (see Figure 5.3). This might confuse a visitor who might try to click on'"dead-end" links. Like page titles and headlines, links shouldn't tease or be coy, ask questions, proffer riddles, or make obscure references (see Figure 5.4).

Like subheads and bullet lists, link text gives impatient visitors to your site a quick way to determine if the page has what they're looking for or if it's a click away. Some experts have gone so far as to say that links are a form of punctuation unique to the hypertext of the Web. Just as starting with a capital letter and ending with a period indicates a sentence, links help indicate to your visitors how the content of your pages and your website is arranged (see Figures 5.5 and 5.6).

A visitor to your site should be able to scan a block of text on a page and know exactly which words and phrases are links. If a visitor has to stare at the page for longer than a second or two to find the links then your links are not clear enough. A visitor should also be able to read the text for a link and get a good idea of what to expect if they click on the link. In this respect you should think about making your links operate like file tabs on a file folder.

Linked images are a different story because the practice of using the default blue border around an image to indicate its "linkedness" has fallen far out of fashion. But there are few other ways that are effective at indicating that an image is linked—a picture may be worth a

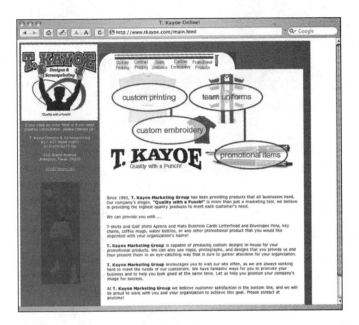

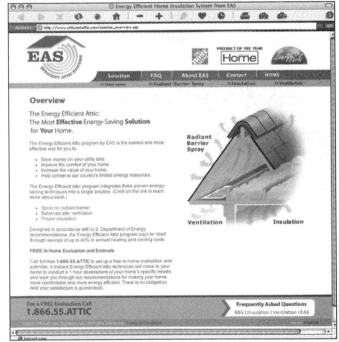

Figure 5.3.
Like Muhammad Ali, the copy on the home page for a marketing products company promotes itself in the extreme (top). Boldfacing the company name every time it appears doesn't emphasize any new information for the visitor. The visitor might think that these highlighted words are links. On the attic insulation website (bottom), meaningful link text stands out on the home page to guide visitors to additional information about the company and its products.

Figure 5.4
The cryptic link titles in this site's main navigation area leave me scratching my head.

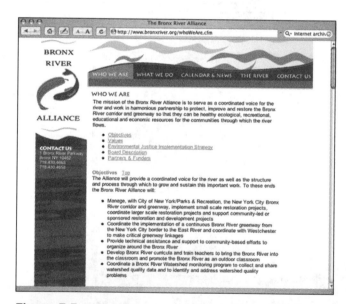

Figure 5.5
A list of links gives a synopsis of the page contents, letting visitors jump to the part they're interested in. Note how well this site uses links like this.

Figure 5.6
The overview page for a placement firm software
application offers a nice balance of images, text as
graphics, and succinct text and meaningful links.

thousand words, but more often than not the words "I am a link" are
not among them. If you want to use a photo or graphic on your site
to link to a pop-up window or another page on your site, make sure
to include an adjacent text link that leads to the same location (see
Figure 5.7). Link title tags can help, too, because they appear only
when the visitors rolls their mouse pointer over a linked image to
show more information, such as "Click thumbnail to see larger version
in pop-up window."

Form Samples and Error Messages

Don't fall into the trap of thinking that a form on your site is like a
Crock-Pot. If you just turn on a form and expect it to do its thing,
you'll get burned, especially if the form is complicated.

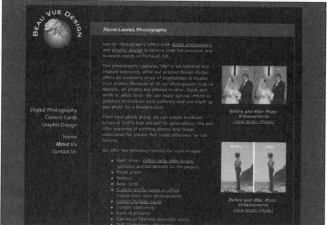

Figure 5.7
On this activities page (top), both the subheads and the images are linked to the same location. On a photographer's site (bottom), a text link below each work sample reiterates that clicking the image opens a larger version in a pop-up window.

A form that doesn't tell visitors how to use it will fail—and you won't even know it. But there are a couple of easy remedies. Make the required fields obvious, with boldface text, an asterisk, or colored background. Or better yet, place some sample input data adjacent to the actual form fields. If you want phone numbers entered with an area code but no parentheses, give an example: 312-555-1212. Use red or another noticeable color and animated or flashing icons to show missing required form fields on a form error page. See the example shown in Figure 5.8 of a website that does this well.

To Search or Not to Search

That is the question. Certainly a small site of three or four pages has no need for a search function. But if you plan to start with more pages or add pages to your site regularly, the ability to search might become a necessity. Fortunately for small site operators, there are several third-party site search engines—FreeFind, Atomz, and even Google—that are cheaper to set up and easier to maintain than running your own search engine on your site.

Figure 5.8
An error message in red paired with flashing red arrowheads indicates the missing information that prevents this form from being submitted.

USE TESTIMONIALS EFFECTIVELY

Testimonials are an excellent choice for small site builders stumped for content to put on their site. They're short (or should be short) and scannable—the perfect bite-size bit of text to put on your page. Testimonials also help connect your site and your business to visitors by helping them vicariously experience the satisfaction they will get from working with you. They're a great way to present an authentic case for why someone should do business with you.

Testimonials are like guilt-free gossip. People love to read what other people say. And as a business owner, soliciting testimonials offers the added benefit of helping you stay in touch with loyal customers. You don't even need to ask for a formal testimonial. If a customer emails you a thank-you such as "As always, we are enjoying working with you. Your service is great!" ask for permission to reword it in the third-person and post it on your site: "We always enjoy working with the folks at Acme Welding. Their service is great!"

Performers, authors, and restaurants should always consider using excerpts from favorable reviews on their sites (see Figure 5.9). Testimonials or product reviews also make a great

There's another approach to consider for sites of less than about 50 pages: a jump menu that lets visitors quickly go from any page on your site to any other with one click. Website authoring software programs like Dreamweaver have built-in tools that can help you quickly build a jump menu for your site. The keys to success with a jump menu are providing meaningful menu choices that match the titles of the pages they link to and a consistent list of choices that does not vary in location or content from page to page.

Other Good Examples of Visual Cues

Here are some other ideas that you should consider to help you create good visual cues:

- Use rollover effects to cause a link, navigation button, or icon on a web page to change in some way when the visitor's mouse pointer passes over it. Good examples include changing the color of the navigation image or making a subtle shift in its position to create a 3D effect. Bad examples include changing the typeface or style with a rollover or a causing a large movement of the underlying image.

- Display a "last-modified" time stamp to reassure (or warn) your visitors about the age of the information on your site. A time stamp can be incorporated into the footer of every page on your site with a simple bit of HTML code.

With your microcontent in order, and the right visual cues in place to help visitors use your site quickly and effectively, you can concentrate on giving visitors to your site what they came for.

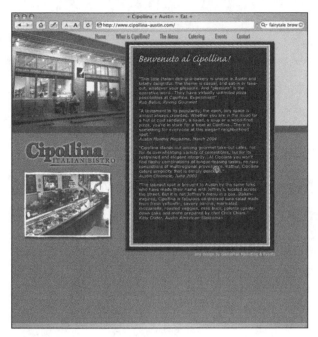

Figure 5.9
Reviews and testimonials are an effective way to persuade visitors to your site that your business can meet their needs. This site shows a good example of how the testimonial text can be set up so that it appears as something special.

Figure 5.10
Limit your testimonials to three to five per page. If you have more, offer a link to a second page.

addition to sites that sell or promote an unusual service or unfamiliar product.

In general, you can republish short excepts from newspapers and magazines without getting permission provided you give the publication credit. As a courtesy, you should always get an individual's consent before quoting them on your site.

Here are some other tips to follow when adding testimonials or reviews to your site:

- Use italics, quotation marks, a box, or colored background to indicate that the testimonial is not ordinary text—it's something special that must be read (see Figure 5.9).

- Set off the name of the person who gave the testimonial with boldface or a slightly larger font size. Link to their company website. Giving special treatment to the attribution signals to visitors that the text is interesting and important and let's them scan the names to see if they know or have heard of any of them.

- As with everything else on a small site, less is more. Three to five testimonials—especially on your home page—are plenty (see Figure 5.10). If you have more than that, offer a link to a subpage with the full list, or categorize the testimonials based on the services or products they pertain to. Also, consider using some kind of JavaScript script to rotate a variety of testimonials on your page (see Figure 5.11).

Figures 5.12 and 5.13 show a few other examples of how testimonials can be set up on a page to highlight them. Whatever approach you take, just make sure that the testimonials really stand out and don't get lost because of clutter on your site.

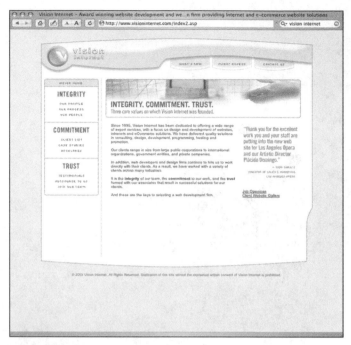

Figure 5.11
A single testimonial on your home page can display a variety of random quotes from satisfied customers using a simple JavaScript.

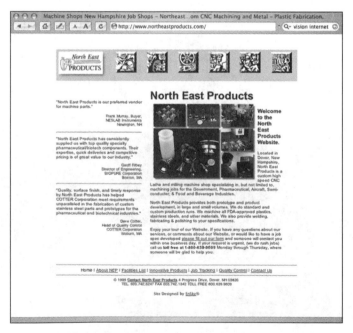

Figure 5.12
I can't endorse the use of such unusual icons on a small site, but the three testimonials on the home page are nicely formatted. Rules separate them and right-justified text sets off the attribution from the quote.

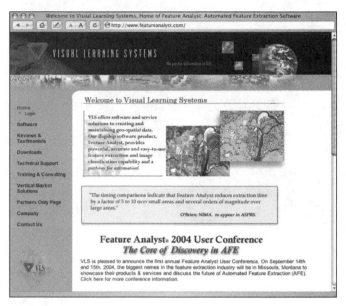

Figure 5.13
A box sets off a single randomly rotated testimonial on a
software company's website.

Websites and Their Dis-Contents

Visitors to your website don't come just to "read" your "content" as
they might a newspaper or a magazine. They are anxious for answers
and goal-oriented. They will scan your web pages for headlines and
links that appear to answer their questions, meet their needs, make
their lives better, or help them do their jobs better. They may even
jump back and forth between two web pages—yours and your competitors'—like an overcaffeinated lab rat. They won't spend the time to
figure things out for themselves; they want web pages to do the thinking for them!

Break Up Your Text So Key Information
Is Easier to Find

The content of your small website is best arranged like an iceberg.
Icebergs, for the three readers out there who did not see *Titanic*, conceal
90 percent of their volume below the ocean's surface. According to the
"iceberg theory of website organization," great small sites give out a
little information at a time—one idea per page.

The "tip of the iceberg" is a succinct glimpse of what lies beyond the
home page, for example, or a search results page (see Figure 5.14).
Visitors who wish to dive in and get more can do so with a thumbnail

USING COMPLEX ELEMENTS LIKE TABLES, MAPS, AND ICONS

Adding more elaborate graphical elements like tables, maps, and icons can give your small site a professional look that sets it apart from other sites. When used correctly, they give a site a graceful quality that augments your visitor's experience.

I'll give you some tips, techniques, and examples for how and when to use advanced design components on your site.

TABLES

Since the Web had its birth in academia, its inventors added table tags to the HTML language as a way to display rows and columns of research data. But web designers far away from any ivory tower quickly discovered that the same rows and columns could hold layout elements such as links and images. They began using page-sized tables to lock design elements in place. Tables remain a tried-and-true web design technique, even as newer HTML technologies such as cascading style sheets and layers make near-pixel perfect layouts possible without tables.

Smaller tables embedded in the main layout table (or placed in a modern CSS-based, table-free layout) also remain a great

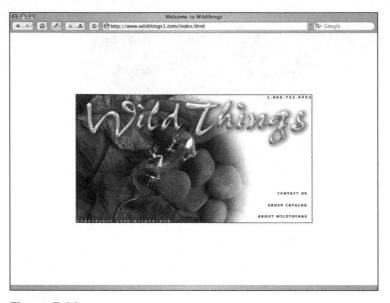

Figure 5.14
"Iceberg right ahead!" This home page keeps options to a minimum.

that links to a larger image or a list of links that leads to more information farther down the page or on a subpage. Disinterested parties (and salty seafarers) can steer clear and move on.

Prepare the information for your website the way you would prepare a meal for a small child: cut up the information into bite-sized pieces, and don't be afraid to spoon-feed it or repeat yourself more than once if you have to.

Considering the difficulty of reading on low-resolution monitors and the short attention span of the typical web surfer, you should limit your content to one topic or concept per page. Instead of having an overview of your products, ordering information, *and* your return policy all on one page, break up the information into three pages.

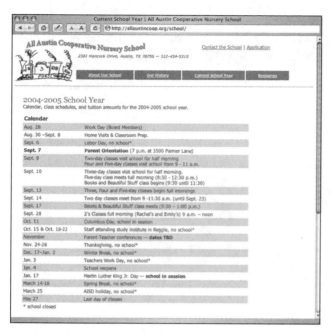

Figure 5.15
A preschool website uses a table with alternating rows that match the site's color scheme to list the upcoming school year's important dates and events.

Figure 5.16
The website for U.S. Felt displays its production schedules in month tables and a color-coded key—another table—at the bottom of the page.

way to display information in an attention-getting, scannable way (see Figures 5.15 and 5.16). Instead of burying your price list, hours of operation, shipping rate card, or performance schedule in plain vanilla text, reformat it in a table with alternating row colors and boldface text to make it really stand out.

MAPS

A lot people visit a small site looking for one thing: a map. If your business is in a hard-to-find location or you get a lot of one-time or walk-in business at your location, a map can be a valuable addition to your site.

Maps also can be used to show multiple business locations in your city or region (see Figure 5.17) or your service area across one or more states (see Figure 5.18).

Online maps that are simple and uncluttered are usually better than intricate, detailed, or colorful maps. If your budget allows, have your web designer stylize your map with color accents and typeface to match the rest of your site (see Figure 5.19).

Government agencies like the U.S. Geological Survey and municipal websites are good sources of public domain maps that you can alter to match your site's color scheme or simplify to highlight your business's location. Usage restrictions on maps from online sources such as

MapQuest may prevent you from altering the map.

Finally, make your map big enough to view and understand on a web page but not so big that it can't be printed intact on a standard, letter-sized sheet of paper. You can use arrows or colored lines to highlight the best route to your business from a major landmark or intersection (see Figure 5.20), but text directions often work just as well.

ICONS

Icons are like spices you add to your web pages—a little goes a long way. You're asking for trouble if you use stand-alone icons for your main site navigation. The 20x20 pixel blob that looks like a catalog to you and your web designer (because you've both seen it a thousand times) won't lead as many visitors to your product pages as a simpler text or graphical link that reads "Catalog." But in specific situations, small icons can really jazz up your pages.

For example, they're great for indicating that a link will download a file. Use an arrow (see Figure 5.21) or a small file-specific icon (Microsoft Word, Adobe PDF).

Small icons or dingbats also can subtly enhance the contact

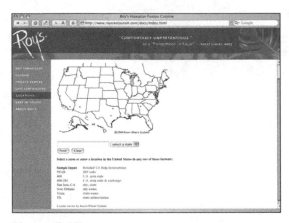

Figure 5.17
Two ways to find locations for this restaurant chain: a clickable map *and* a search form, with sample search entries provided.

Figure 5.18
The Mead Equipment website combines its contact information with a map that pinpoints its headquarters and defines its service area.

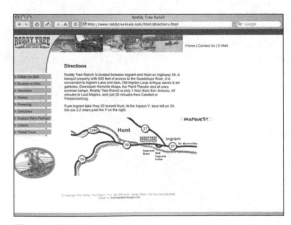

Figure 5.19
This summer camp marks it location on a map with its logo.

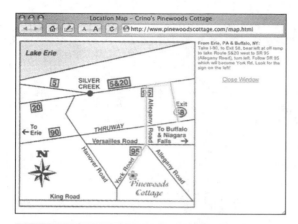

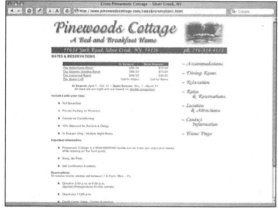

information on your site. They'll look even better if you or your designer spend the time to rework them for the same size, proportion, and color scheme. Using a limited color palette or monochromatic icons looks classier than slapping three clip-art icons on your page in hopes of achieving a good design (see Figures 5.22 and 5.23).

Figure 5.20
The Pinewood Cottages website (bottom) offers a larger map in a pop-up window (top) and highlights a preferred route in yellow.

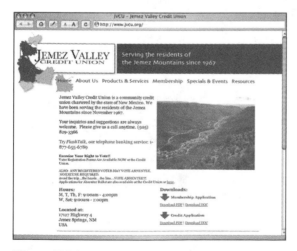

Figure 5.21
Arrows highlight the download section of this credit union home page.

Figure 5.22
Use icons that share a color scheme and can set off and call attention to the address and phone number listing on your website.

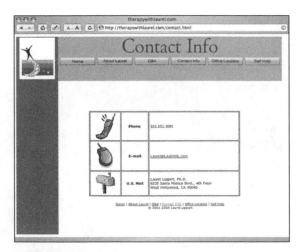

Figure 5.23
Clip-art icons make a site look unpolished.

Keep Paragraphs Short—One Idea per Paragraph

But don't just fill your pages with strings of one-idea paragraphs. Long blocks of text can induce a phenomenon known among professionals as "eyes glazing over." Use bullet lists and subheads to give your visitors' eyes something to jump to as they scan the page. Group two or three related paragraphs under a subhead (see Figure 5.24). Or if you have a list of services or products in a paragraph of text, break it out with bullets and use a subhead to introduce the list (see Figure 5.25).

Figure 5.24
Subheads and short paragraphs give an easy-to-read overview of this product's potential uses.

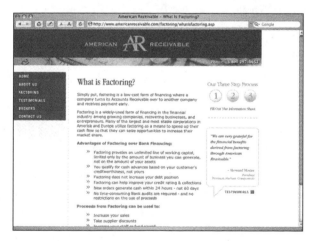

Figure 5.25
Bullet lists and subheads make this page easy to digest.

Write (or Rewrite) Tight Copy for Scannability

If you have copy that's already written, it's likely in the form of a brochure or some other marketing collateral. Websites based on brochures, known by the pejorative "brochureware," have been given a bad wrap. One reason is that the early adopters of the Web wanted to move on to something else. But peering beyond the prejudice, brochure copy just doesn't make good website copy. Your website can serve the same purpose as your printed brochure, but the content has to be formatted for the unique requirements of the Web.

If you're starting with brochure copy or any other source material that was written for print—white papers, price sheets, a media kit—strip it down to the topic sentence of each paragraph and then go back and fill in just the crucial blanks (see Figure 5.26). Try to keep the result to around 30 to 50 percent of its original length. Consider offering a downloadable version of your complete brochure for those who want to know more.

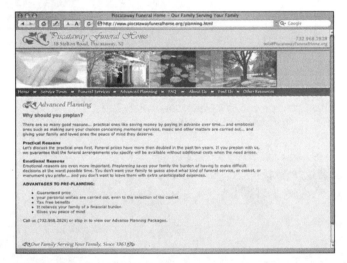

Figure 5.26
A succinct page on a complicated subject—planning your own funeral—keeps visitors to this site from feeling overwhelmed.

If you don't have any copy for your site (or if what you have ain't so good), where can you get some "good content? " Don't feel compelled to write the Great American Novel for your website. Write short, scannable blurbs or lists to fill the pages. Keep the text per page to fewer than 500 words. As with page titles and headlines, avoid jokes or anecdotes in your writing. Make it as straightforward as possible.

Most visitors to your site are looking for one piece of information. Once they find it, they may be receptive to getting more. But don't overwhelm them with everything at once.

Microcontent can't bloat your site, but too much content, obscure functionality, or both can. Pages filled with text and complex multimedia presentations mean time spent proofreading and updating. Poorly planned or unnecessary functionality can lead to endless troubleshooting with emails and phone calls. Instead, keep the content and functionality on your site simple, small, and manageable—bite-sized—and you won't get bitten.

Summary

In this chapter, you learned that content and functionality together give visitors to your site the important information they're seeking about your business. You saw how functionality can lead your site visitors to the content they're seeking.

Website content must be succinct: Subheads, bullet lists, and short text blurbs are among the easy-to-employ formatting techniques that can turn dull, dense text into engaging and scannable web pages.

You also learned about the important role of microcontent in binding content and functionality together. Even simple, fundamental functionality like a contact form or jump menu requires informative page titles, meaningful link text, and attention to other content details in order to effectively deliver your website's message to your visitors and potential customers.

Together with the right focus, design format, and navigation scheme, content and functionality combine to create the complete small site package. Whether yours has just one page or twenty pages, the perfect marriage of these components yields a website that produces results for your business: increased interest from new customers, word-of-mouth marketing from loyal customers, and time and expense saved because your website can be more efficient at communicating and transacting business with your customers than phone, email, or personal contact.

In the next section, we'll turn our attention to taking your small site to the next level with successful marketing strategies that follow the Small Site philosophy by helping you bring the right visitors to your site and win them over as customers.

SMALL SITE APPROACH TO WEB MARKETING

6

- Learn how to leverage your existing marketing efforts and create new ways for customers to interact with your small site.

- Learn that low-budget, word of mouth marketing is the way to go, especially for small sites.

- Learn proven techniques for offline to online marketing, online to online marketing, and online to offline marketing.

Contrary to popular opinion, marketing your business with your website means more than search engine placement and page rankings. Marketing is about getting people—the right people, not just lots of them—to visit your site. And once they are at your site, good follow-up marketing gets them to take some type of action, such as purchase a product or request a quote.

Recall from Chapter 3 that I defined a focused website as one that puts your customers' needs and interests first. Focus creates boundaries between the types of content and navigation that are right for your site and those that are not.

A small, focused, and well-maintained website can complement your other marketing activities. A website offers an advantage over other marketing activities. Where advertising, junk mail, and other marketing messages may be perceived as intrusive (even disingenuous), potential customers who find your website have done so voluntarily. A bloated site will seem out of step with your other marketing efforts and end up turning away potential customers.

In this chapter I'll be focusing on the first key phase of marketing—attracting solid leads and customers. In the next chapter we'll turn our attention to actually turning site visitors into loyal customers.

Why Marketing for Small Sites?

You might be thinking, "I don't do any marketing—just an occasional flyer or coupon mailer or yellow pages ad." You might also be thinking, "I really don't need to do any marketing because my site and my business are small." And of course, if you are like most small site and small business owners, you might feel that you can't do any marketing because you don't have the money to spend. Marketing is probably the last thing on your mind, especially if you have bills to pay, other work to get done, and a website that still needs to be updated.

The reality is that without marketing, your website and business will eventually fall into a rut. You may currently have a set of customers who are fueling the growth of your business, but without a continued source of new customers, you likely won't have a sustainable business. Fortunately, the Web can offer you a number of outlets and techniques for marketing your business in a highly targeted and cost-effective manner.

As we start to discuss marketing, it's important to understand that marketing isn't limited to just advertising. According to **www.MarketingProfs.com**, a website for marketing professionals and educators, "Public relations, media planning, product pricing and distribution, sales strategy, customer support, market research, and community involvement are all parts of comprehensive marketing efforts." Even if your site is small, you should have a good plan in place that involves different marketing efforts so that you can grow your customer base and improve your chances of success, as you'll learn in this chapter.

Marketing encompasses every way that the name of your business gets in front of the eyes of your customers and potential customers. When you're building a small site, all your offline marketing efforts provide ways to introduce your website as a place for people to get more information about your business or get a special offer from your business.

In return, a properly maintained and updated website can strengthen your other marketing efforts. With its self-service, always-on attributes, your website offers a cost-effective way to extend—and even track—your other marketing efforts without extending your budget.

If you are building a small site, you likely have a small business and you need to be as smart as you can about your marketing. Marketing can get very expensive and wasteful unless you really know how to leverage the resources and tools that are available to you both online and offline.

Complementary Marketing

Making your small site work with your other marketing activities is really critical and thus is where you should start. This is an important strategy that you should never lose sight of no matter how much your site grows or how significant it becomes in relation to your overall business. The one important lesson we've all learned (or should have learned) over the past few years is that the Web (and Web businesses) can't operate in a sort of "online vacuum." Customers don't just live in online communities—they shop in stores, go to work, go to school, entertain themselves at ball games, and engage in a myriad of other activities. The best marketing efforts should be designed to reach customers in multiple ways, creating a powerful but consistent message.

More importantly, successful complementary marketing efforts use response devices that encourage people to take action. If you offer prospective customers a free consultation or estimate in exchange for finding out about their interest in your business, you're already engaged in a kind of response-oriented marketing (see Figure 6.1). Other familiar examples include postage-paid subscription cards or envelopes in magazines and toll-free numbers on late-night infomercials for quirky mail-order products.

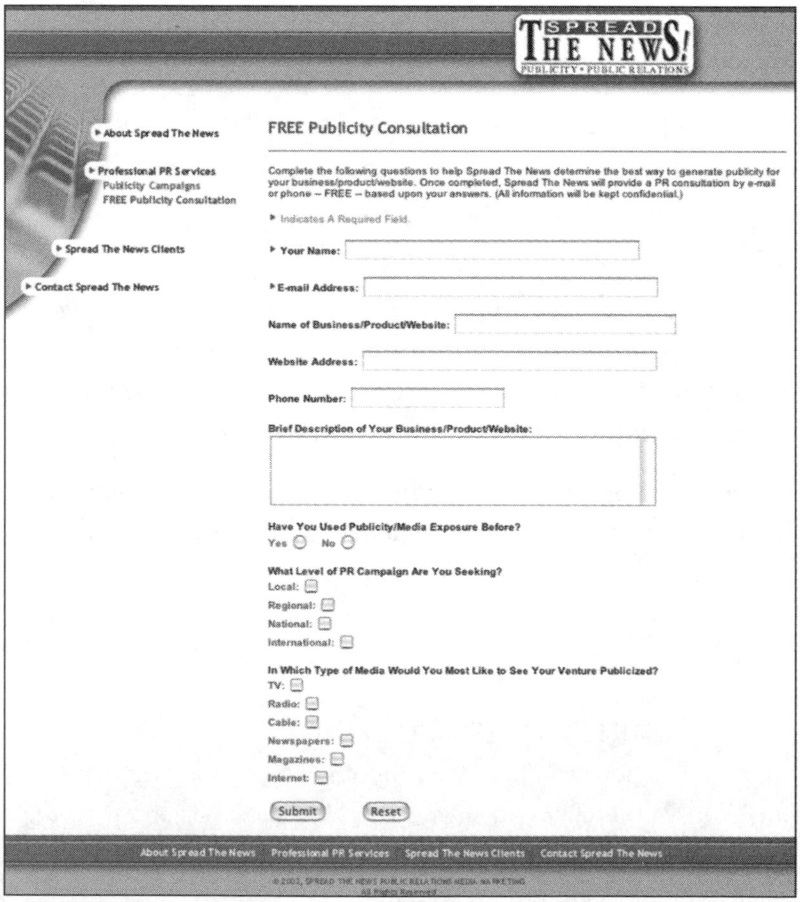

Figure 6.1
Adding a few well-chosen questions and the word *free* changes a simple contact form into something of value for visitors and a source of leads for your business.

Online response devices prompt visitors to your site to take an action to become more involved with your business or prompt offline customers to visit your website. Good ones are easy to set up, easy to remember and use, easy to track, and easy to change.

Your website should be geared toward leveraging your existing marketing efforts and creating new ways for customers to respond to you with their interest in your business. When you're website enters the marketing equation, modes of response fall into three categories: offline to online, online to offline, and—the most important—online to online. Let's look at each of these approaches next.

Offline to Online Marketing

The best way to encourage offline to online response (i.e., getting people to visit your website) is to put your website address on everything: business cards, menus, signs, ads, and postcards—even printed receipts and invoices. A better idea is to give people a specific reason to visit your website: to sign-up for your email list, find out about new products and offers, or heaven knows what else (see Figure 6.2).

Figure 6.2
An e-prayer request form, located in the lower-left corner of the home page, gives visitors to this Oregon church website the ultimate portal.

Let's look more specifically at how your website can complement the more common facets of offline to online marketing, such as advertising, direct mail, customer support, sale pricing, and community outreach.

- **Don't ignore the yellow pages**. Most people still turn to the local yellow pages when they are looking for a business or resource. Instead of simply listing your phone number, as everyone else does, you should prominently display your website address and encourage potential customers to use the Web. You could mention that you provide special offers at your website or that you provide special information. For example, if you are a plumber, you might indicate in your yellow pages ad that you have information on your website designed to help customers deal with emergency problems. Because the yellow pages are jam-packed with other businesses and services that likely compete with yours, it's important to offer something that makes your business really stand out from the pack. Most businesses forget to mention that they even have a website because their ads are cluttered with trying to list all of the services that they provide. Featuring your website, especially if your business is the type that usually attracts customers who use the Internet, can give you a competitive advantage.

- **Specialty advertising**. If you want your advertising efforts to draw more people to your site, consider paying extra for placement in the Web-specific classifieds, a section of many newspapers that highlights the websites of small business. Provide an auto-responder address—as well as your website address—that people can use to receive more information by email.

  You should also consider advertising in specialty publications, which are often cost effective. In many towns, there are often specialty guides for travel and tourism, restaurant reviews, home building, real estate, arts and entertainment, and so on. These are ideal for promoting your business and your website because you can readily reach a highly targeted audience.

- **Promote customer service**. In the realm of customer support, including your website address on product information sheets, instructions, and catalogs can reinforce the utility and customer-oriented focus of your business and your website. And when you can't address your customers' questions or problems by phone, include your website address on your telephone voice message or call-routing phone system. This way, people can reach you 24/7. If they call your number and you are not there, you can direct them to a website that can answer specific questions they might have. If you have the type of phone system that allows you to provide information for different departments (e.g., "press 2 to reach customer service"), you can provide a specific website address for the appropriate area of your website that corresponds with the phone department a customer has selected. This approach allows you to focus your customer service efforts and save your customers valuable time.

- **Offer deals**. People love to get deals, especially when they're surfing the Web. You can take advantage of the discount-hunter mentality by using your website to tweak your pricing and sales strategy. You can inexpensively distribute coupons door to door or in community mailers. (When you use coupons, it is a good idea to always include an expiration date. This encourages customers to follow through and take some action.)

  You can use the print advertising and coupons you circulate to mention special offers and deals customers can obtain by going to your website. Offer people the opportunity to download and print more coupons from your website from a special web address that you provide. You might even go so far as to advertise that you have something like a "Special Offer of the Week" program to encourage customers to come to your website. The important thing is to make any specials you provide really stand out from those offered by your competitors.

  Because of the dynamic nature of the Web, you can easily try out different offers to see which gets the best response from your customers. You could pass out flyers in different parts of town, each providing a different website address to access a special offer that is slightly different. Strategies like this can help save you time and money in fine-tuning your marketing and promotions.

- **Public relations efforts**. Your public relations or community relations efforts might take on new importance when you see the potential they have for building traffic to your website. When your small site is launched or redesigned, send a news release to local media outlets. Better yet, find out if your local television newscasts feature a website of the day or week and propose that the next one

CHOOSING THE RIGHT
DOMAIN NAME FOR
YOUR SITE

According to statistics compiled by Name Intelligence, Inc. and listed at **www.whois.sc**, there are more than 30 million active dot-com domain names. Tens of thousands of new ones are registered every day. And those numbers do not even include less popular—but still actively traded—top-level domains like .org and .biz, whose numbers collectively total in the millions.

Will the domain you want to register for your business be available? Maybe, or maybe not, depending on how common your business name is. Most web hosting providers will check the availability of your domain name choice and may even offer to register it for you for free when you sign up for a hosting plan.

If you're undecided about which domain name to use or have to settle for something less than your first choice, your main concern should be on choosing a domain name that is memorable, easy to say, and easy to spell. If yourname.com is taken, then yourname.net, yourname.biz, yourname.info, and youname.us are worthy alternatives to consider. Here are some other tips to keep in

be yours. If you're the charitable type and donate your business's products or services to local causes, ask the receiving organizations to publish your website address in their newsletters or link back to your site from their websites.

Online to Offline Marketing

Response devices can also work in reverse by prompting visitors to your website to visit your physical location or otherwise contact you personally. The mailing list you promote on your website doesn't have to be a virtual one. Letting people request a printed catalog or sign up for your postal mailing list is just as legitimate a use for a small site as an online shopping cart or email list is.

Likewise, just because your time and budget doesn't allow for e-commerce doesn't mean you can't start the point-of-sale process online and finish it offline. A downloadable in-store coupon (see Figure 6.3) and the aforementioned free consultation are good ways to convert your website visitors into walk-in customers. On your website, you can take your free consultation a step further by asking visitors to complete an online survey in exchange for a free consultation or discount on their first order or appointment with your business. Artists, performers, and consultants can use regular site updates to alert their fans and followers about upcoming shows, performances, readings, or workshops.

Meanwhile, on the cutting edge of our increasingly virtual world, communities of political activists and pranksters in the United States and elsewhere have used novel online techniques to influence offline events. The examples range from the recently completed presidential campaign—where sites like **moveon.org** facilitated real-world "meet-ups" of like-minded politicos—to urban "smart mobs" organized by text messaging and mobile phone "trees." While it remains to be seen if such guerilla tactics will have mainstream marketing applications, they nonetheless demonstrate the Internet's capacity to influence groups of people in a cheap and efficient manner with tools that are available to almost everyone.

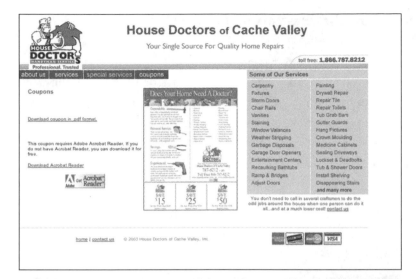

Figure 6.3
Offering downloadable in-store coupons on your site turns Web traffic into foot traffic. A thumbnail of the coupon lends legitimacy to the offer.

Online to Online Marketing

Marketing to people who are already online—with your website just a click away—is the best way to build interest to your site and to increase traffic. Web directory listings and email newsletters, both of which I'll cover in the next sections, are valuable vehicles for this type of marketing. Also, consider providing a simple link on your site that lets visitors email a link to your website to someone else. The "send to a friend" feature has the added advantage of using your existing website visitors' influence with their friends to build your website's traffic and, hopefully, your customer base.

mind when choosing a domain name for your site:

- Try to find a name that matches or complements your business name. Your main marketing goal with your business should be to always promote its name. If the name of your business is too general (like AAA Tires) and the website name is taken, try to select a name that complements a unique feature of your business or a marketing slogan that your business is known for. For example, our friends at AAA Tires are known for selling tires without hassles, so a good website name for them might be **www.tireswithout hassles.com**. If you use this approach, make sure that you select a name (and marketing slogan) that you are prepared to live with for a long time. In other words, really think it through.

- Leave out hyphens, especially if you hope to send a lot of traffic to your site from phone calls or via your outgoing voice mail message. Web surfers have long since gotten used to the Web's peculiar grammar, so don't feel compelled to replace spaces in your business name with a hyphen. That little horizontal bar looks small and innocuous, but it takes almost twice as long to say a domain with one as it does to say a domain name without one. Try it: Say "**acmewelding.com**" and "**acme-welding.com**."

- Avoid long acronyms. Four letters is about as many as I can remember when a company has reduced its website address to an unfamiliar acronym—and I may not remember them in the correct order. A physicians practice in Las Vegas called the Center for Diseases and Surgery of the Spine has a website at **www.cdsslv.com**. A better choice would have been **www.lasvegasspine center.com**.

- Leave out extraneous filler terms like *inc, co, llc,* and *andassoc.* The .com is short for *commercial,* so the extra corporate affirmation is redundant.

- Make sure your web host enables connections to your site both with the "www" and without before printing your domain name on business cards, menus, brochures, and other collateral material.

In addition to your main website address, you might also consider registering alternate addresses. At 5 to 10 dollars a year, domains aren't particularly expensive, but the fees can add

Integrate Your Site with Effective Email Marketing

Even in this era of spam overload, collecting email addresses from visitors to your site and sending a regular message can play an important role in building the right kind of traffic to your site. People who've given you permission to communicate with them about your business—to market to them—constitute a rich vein of new and repeat business.

If you're going to do an email newsletter, keep in mind that doing so is an exercise in publishing. You need to follow the same standards for designing, writing, proofreading, and testing an email newsletter that you would when building and maintaining your website:

- **Make it easy for people to subscribe**. All you really need is an email address, so put a link to the sign-up form, or the sign-up form itself (a small simple text field for collecting an email address) on every page of your website.

- **Keep you email newsletter short and to the point**. No one wants to read a long-winded email newsletter, no matter how loyal a customer they may be. Make sure the content offers your subscribers something of value.

- **Email newsletters come in two formats: text and HTML**. If you want your newsletter to have the same graphical look as your site, work with a web designer who has experience creating HTML newsletters (see Figure 6.4), or spend the time yourself to test your message in the more popular email clients, such as Outlook, Lotus, Eudora, and AOL.

- **If you're managing a small email list yourself, put instructions for unsubscribing in every message you send**. And make a backup of your mailing list once in a while.

- **Put a sample copy of your email newsletter (preferably the latest edition) on your website**. This will allow people to read it to see what they're going to get if they subscribe.

- **Create special pages or even directories on your site that are linked only from your emails**. Doing so will make tracking statistics for your message's effectiveness easier.

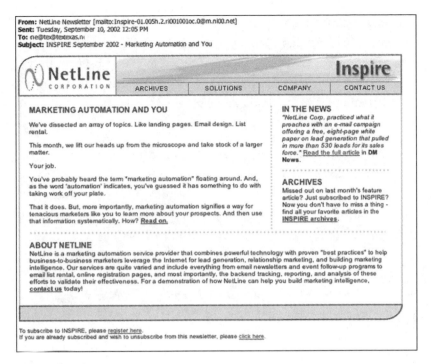

Figure 6.4
HTML email newsletters can display colors, graphics, and links like a web page. Good ones offer a plain text alternative for subscribers who can't or don't want to receive the enhanced version and clear instructions for unsubscribing (lower left).

Small Site Search-Engine Strategies

Search engine and web directory listings are another big part of online to online web marketing.

While search engine ranking is not the be-all and end-all marketing strategy for a small business with a website, you will want to spend some time fine-tuning your site so it will be picked up by search engines. You'll also want to spend some money to be listed with the major web directories, such as Yahoo! and LookSmart.

There are a few things you should know about search-engine ranking. Getting to the top of the rankings takes time, money, or both (usually both). And there's almost always someone willing to spend more of both to beat you to the top of the search results for your market or product.

up, especially for a small business with a limited marketing budget that might be better spent on something else. Here are some ideas and guidelines to follow if you're thinking about stocking up on domain names:

- Register specialty domains that fit your profession. Thanks to international agreements, doctors (and others) now have the option of registering .md domains (thanks, Moldova!). A TV repair shop can claim acmerepair.tv (thanks, Tuvalu!). A good web hosting company should keep you apprised of new top-level domains like these that can be hosted on your account.

- Protect your trademark or business name from cyber squatters. But keep in mind that your business is not a multinational bull's-eye like McDonald's Corp., which has a real need to register all the permutations of its name that it can and the deep pockets to do it.

- Juice up your online presence with a catchy domain name to make your website more noticeable. A psychologist friend of mine in Los Angeles has a site at **lashrink.com**.

Trying to outthink the methods Google uses to index the Web (the legendary "Google algorithm") has become big business, with its practitioners charging thousands of dollars to optimize a website for the best search-engine ranking. You could buy your own search-engine simulation software—a common tool of search-engine specialists—but that would cost you nearly as much as hiring a consultant.

And even if you find yourself at the top of the heap (and smoke is coming out of your web server), more traffic to your website doesn't mean more paying customers. You're better off turning a thousand visits to your website into 20 or 30 new customers or prospects through referrals, response devices, and repeat visits than getting twice as many by engineering a traffic spike with every optimization trick in the book. The extra bandwidth and disk space charges that will accompany your website's popularity (plus the time and money you'll spend) can easily wipe out the gains from the additional sales.

Using Meta Tags

So how should you make search-engine optimization and ranking part of your strategy for getting the word out about your website without spending all your money and time in the process? Start by attending to the details that should already be part of a good website's construction: the meta tags and microcontent that we covered in Chapter 5.

Of the dozen or so types of meta tags that are part of the official HTML specification, the ones that matter most to how your site is indexed and ranked are the description and keywords meta tags. The contents of these tags do not appear on your web pages. They exist simply to give search engines and web directories a synopsis of a website and guidance on how to index it, sort of like the library cataloging information that appears on the copyright page of most books.

The description tag should be about two dozen words that explain your company in plain English. The keywords tag is a series of comma-separated phrases that expand on the description tag and (ideally) anticipate the search terms people will use when they go looking for a business like yours (see Figure 6.5). Character limits for the keywords tag vary among the major search engines (and some ignore them altogether), so you can include as many as you want. But don't bother with single-word entries, and make sure you arrange your keyword list with the most important phrases at the top rather than alphabetically.

Figure 6.5
The HTML code view of thebarstoolshop.com's home page (left) shows keyword and description tags that do not appear on the actual home page (middle). But their power is evident on Google, where the site appears in the first page of results in a search for one of the site's keyword choices: "unique wooden barstools."

Also, write informative and, wherever possible, enticing titles for your home page and other pages on your website (see Figure 6.6). Window titles—the words that appear in the title bar of the browser window when the page loads—are the words that will be linked in the search results. Try to use one or two of your best keyword phrases in the titles of your site's most important pages.

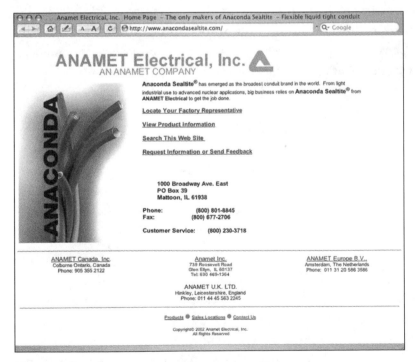

Figure 6.6
The Anamet Electrical website page titles cover the necessary basics—company name and page location—and offer a concise description of what makes the business unique.

Pay at the Register

Take the time to submit your website manually to the directories you can afford rather than relying on all-in-one submission sites or services. In other words, if you want it done right, do it yourself.

Getting a listing on all the major web directories, such as Yahoo! and MSN, can cost $600 to $700, with some sites requiring an annual renewal. (Many web directories offer a reduced fee or free listing for nonprofit and noncommercial sites.) For a list of the specific fees, visit **www.affinityresources.com/pgs/seo.html** or the individual directories.

Google offers an inexpensive advertising program, called AdWords, that can give your search result placement an extra boost. With AdWords, you can create an account and enter some search terms for your business. Then when someone searches for the keywords you've entered, your website and business tagline appear in a small highlighted box next to the other search results. It's inexpensive and you get charged for only the number of times your keywords come up in a search. (Even if you don't run an AdWords ad, the AdWords keyword suggestion tool is a good way to compile and hone your keywords list based on Google's own estimate of how often a phrase gets searched.) Sponsored links on web directories are also worth a look if your budget will allow, but nothing beats AdWords in bang for the buck.

Tell It with Text

The search-engine robots that "spider" the web to continuously update their indexes of the world's websites feed on text. Unlike your computer's web browser, which has plug-ins and add-ons for viewing content in non-text formats, spiders get tripped up on navigation menus that require JavaScript to display or content that requires Java applets or Flash to load dynamically on the page.

I'm a fan of using JavaScript for creating dynamic HTML effects like drop-down menus—and my opinion about Flash has been covered elsewhere in this book. So if you or your web designer are committed to using any of these tools on your site, a site map (which I asserted earlier can be a challenge to keep up-to-date) provides an alternate way for the indexing robots to get all the links on your site in one big bite. With a link to your site map on your home page, you can use

JavaScript or (gulp) Flash or Java on your site and know that it won't keep the search-engine spiders from finding the rest of the pages on your site.

Market Your Site with a Network of Other Like Sites

Links from other sites to yours carry a lot of weight in determining your search result rankings. If your site is considered worth mentioning on another website, then your site must be valuable—or so the search-engine thinking goes.

What types of sites should you try to get listed on? The easy ones are the ones that already cater to people or businesses with your credentials or specialization. Good candidates to start with include professional directories; trade school, technical school, or college alumni directories; and town, city, or neighborhood directories. So pay your association dues to get listed on your peer group's website and make a habit of asking regular customers to promote your services on local web directories, especially ones that feature recommended businesses.

If your business offers a particular amenity, service, or product that's uncommon among your competitors, seek out a listing on the web directories that specialize in tracking establishments like yours. Examples include bed and breakfasts that take pets, ice cream shops with free wireless Internet access, banquet halls that serve vegetarian meals, and repair shops that specialize in foreign brands.

Complementary businesses are another source of shared links. A massage therapist who frequently recommends the services of her friend the acupuncturist, hypnotist, or yoga instructor should have a link to her colleague's website, and vice versa. Before you approach anyone about linking to your site, though, you should create your own links page where you can reciprocate with a link back to them.

Getting the rest of the world to link to your website takes a bit more effort. You can build interest in your site by featuring compelling content that gets updated regularly. You might think that takes time and money, and in most cases you'd be right. Instead, think small: Consistency and clarity-not quantity and complexity—are the keys to maintaining a small site with fresh content.

With a little imagination, a small weekly, or even monthly, change on your site can lure all manner of special interest groups with a concern for what your website says. For example, an HVAC installer who offers a seasonal maintenance tip might draw links from do-it-yourselfer websites. A weekly coupon or Web-only special gets the attention of the deal-tracking sites frequented by bargain hunters.

Even clever, targeted, low-cost strategies for marketing your business through your website take time to bear fruit, so be persistent and patient with your efforts. You can't get a hundred websites to link to your site until you get the first one to do it.

Likewise, you can't beat a hundred sites to the top of the Google rankings without spending a fortune. Creators of small sites can't afford to let search-engine optimization turn into search-engine obsession.

Let your website's focus guide your marketing efforts toward finding and attracting the right visitors.

Summary

In this chapter, you learned how your offline and online marketing activities should complement one another to have the best combined impact on the success of your business. I first explained creative strategies for promoting your business offline with an eye to getting your customers to come to your website. We then looked at some useful techniques for promoting your business in reverse—using your website to promote your business offline. Finally, we looked at many of the techniques and tools that are helpful for using search engines and other websites to promote and market your business.

In the next chapter, I'll expand on what you learned in this chapter and explore ways in which you can use your small site to build relationships with your customers so that they keep coming back.

STRATEGIES FOR TURNING VISITORS INTO CUSTOMERS

7

- Learn how to create experiences for your visitors so that they will keep coming back.

- Learn how to design your small site to make it as trustworthy as possible.

- Learn how to encourage visitors to take action and become real customers.

As you learned in Chapter 6, there are a number of marketing techniques you can put to work to attract the right visitors to your small site. But no matter how good you get at attracting visitors, you'll still have more work to do because attracting them is only half the battle of creating a successful small site. Converting first-time visitors into loyal customers requires offering them compelling reasons for staying and returning, establishing a trusting relationship with them, and getting a significant portion of them to show an interest in your business while visiting your website.

In this chapter I'll show you how to take the next step and turn actual visitors into real customers. You'll learn how important it is to build trust with your customers, and I'll provide you with some proven website design techniques that can help build and keep trust. "Designing for trust" is something you rarely read about in books or articles on web design, but it is an important concept that can really help your website (and your business) reach its full potential.

Get Your Visitors' Attention and Keep Them Coming Back

Whether you're drawing millions of visitors to your website every month or just hundreds, you won't get repeat visitors and customers without capturing and retaining the attention of first-timers *and* creating a lasting impression about your business's and site's value that will prompt them to come back. That's a tall order in an online world where every other website is just a click or two away.

A few years ago, a Forrester study of the reasons people return to a website revealed some insights into the priorities of web surfers. At the top of the list were bread-and-butter website qualities like frequently updated, quality content; fast load time and ease of use; and coupons and incentives. Bringing up the rear were the so-called "sticky" website features (i.e., they get people to stick around): e-commerce, games, chat, forums, and other bloatware that unsuccessful websites pile on in hopes of attracting visitors.

Don't confuse getting your visitors' attention with the online equivalent of shouting or showing off. Attention-getting does not require animated GIFs, scrolling text, auto-playing audio or video clips, or any other form of virtual arm-waving. Some sites even use tricks to keep visitors. Some of these tricks include pop-up windows or pop-under windows that appear when a visitor leaves the site or false entry pages that immediately forward the visitor to the real entry page. In the latter case, when a visitor clicks the back button to leave, the false entry page automatically redirects the visitor back to the deceptive site's home page. In reality—as those of you who've read the book straight through should know and the rest of you can surely guess—techniques like this are a can't-miss indication of a bloated site, or worse (see Figure 7.1).

Figure 7.1
The attention-getting antics of a structural foam manufacturer's site include a cryptic Flash-generated thermometer (top left), followed by a dizzying slideshow of words and photos (top middle). The actual home page (top right) features spinning logos, taglines that scroll, and navigation buttons that emit a lightsaber-like "whoosh" when clicked, but few reasons for a potential customer to stay. A similar company's site (bottom) eschews the eye-candy in favor of interesting, well-proportioned home-page sections that really speak to new and returning visitors.

What's more, stunts and "stupid web tricks" grow old on second viewing (midway through the first for some), causing too many visitors to roll their eyes as they roll their mouse over to the back button. That's one of the main arguments against using a Flash intro on a small site: Once it's been seen, no one wants to see it again. You could spend a little extra money to use browser cookies to detect new visitors from repeat visitors and skip the intro for repeat visitors, or better yet, you could just skip the intro altogether.

Getting your visitors' attention is about focusing your site for them, rather than gumming it up with unnecessary gimmicks. That means providing the content and functionality that sustains their interest, speaks their language, and gives them a reason to stay—but doesn't prevent them from leaving if they want to (see Figure 7.1). When I explained the importance of focusing your small site in Chapter 3, I identified what goes through the minds of most of the people who visit a site for the first time:

- Why should I do business with you?

- Will this company be easy to work with or hard to work with?

- Why is this company different from the rest?

- Does this site and this business have what I need? Can I find it quickly?

- And, most importantly, why does this site exist and what can I do here?

Remember, when thinking about your website's focus, people generally have three reasons for visiting:

- **They want to get quick, accurate information about your business.** If the information your visitors are seeking is hard or impossible to find—even if the reason is unintentional—they might assume that your business has something to hide. Or they might think that your business is not customer focused and that you don't really care if your customers have a good experience. We've all had dealings with businesses (and websites) that have attitudes like this, and our first reaction is to run away.

- **They want to interact or communicate with you or other customers.** On a more basic level, your visitors may be wondering if you even *have* any customers. What is the online equivalent of the framed dollar bill behind the shopkeeper's counter? Things like a list of frequently asked questions, clear shipping and return policies, and testimonials from satisfied customers offer proof that you have anticipated your customers' problems and questions.

- **They want to transact business with you on their schedule.** The advantage of a website is it's there for your potential customers when you aren't. But it also has to tell them when *you're* there for them by clearly indicating your business and phone support hours. Don't send your potential customers into a frustrating feedback loop, where your site instructs them to call anytime and your outgoing voice mail message instructs people to visit your site.

If your site doesn't impress visitors with clear and intuitive ways to meet those needs and answer their questions, then many first visits will be last visits as well.

Establishing Trust for Your Site (and Business)

Getting your website visitors to pay attention to your website is just the first step in turning website traffic into website success. Your website also must demonstrate both with what it says and with how it's run that you and your business can be trusted. Being the last frontier (for now) of get-rich-quick schemes, scams, and spams, the Internet leaves a lot to be desired in the reliability department. Viruses, email worms, and buggy software add to the perception that everything that has to do with computers (and especially the Internet) is suspect.

Today, criminal activity, such as identity theft, is at an all-time high. The extreme amount of spam and other aggressive rip-off techniques like "phishing" have made the Internet an unsafe place for many. Therefore, the typical new visitor to your site will likely come to you with a list of the following uncertainties:

- Can I actually trust this site or business? In other words, is this business really legitimate?

- Has this business been around for any length of time and will it likely stay in business?

- Is the business financially sound?

- Is the business under any duress, legal or otherwise?

- Is the business run out of a storefront, office, or someone's kitchen?

- What kinds of customers does the business attract?

- Does it have much experience in offering the products and services that it is currently offering?

- Am I dealing with a full-time or part-time business?

- Would it be safe to order a product from this site? Can I trust that the products are actually in stock?

- Will my personal information (credit card number, phone number, and so on) be kept confidential?

- Will my email address be given out to annoying spammers or others that could do me real harm?

- Does the business really follow its privacy policy?

- If I purchase a product, will it be shipped on time?

- If I have a problem with a product that I ordered, what can I do?

- Will there be anyone around to answer the phone if I need to call for customer assistance?

- If I have a bad experience working with this site, is there anything else I can do about it?

Many people simply won't buy products or services from websites unless they already have some type of relationship with the business outside of the Internet. For example, if customers already purchase products from a retail store, they might feel comfortable ordering products from the company's website.

If you have a web business that does not have an offline presence, you'll need to work more diligently to build and keep trust. Fortunately, as you'll learn in this chapter, there are a number of techniques that you can apply to build trust.

Designing for Trust

A number of books have been published on the art of designing websites to make them look cool or to make them more useable. But the real art of designing a small business website involves creating a sense of trust for the customer, who when using the Web will often need to purchase products or services sight unseen. Designing for trust involves understanding the mindset of the customer and finding direct ways to address the concerns that the customer might have. For example, if you make custom shoes and have a small site to sell them, there are certain features you could emphasize on your site:

- Your shoes are made from the finest leather available (but only state something like this if it is really true).

- You guarantee every pair of shoes you sell. If a customer is not satisfied with a pair, you'll allow them to return the shoes with no questions asked.

- You promise to ship every order in 24 to 48 hours. You should also always notify the customer when their shoes have been shipped.

- Customers can contact you at any time to track an order that has been shipped.

These are just a few of the types of commitments that you can make to help customers trust your website and business. To help you incorporate some practical design ideas, I'll show you how to build trust by using special content on your site and by performing certain types of actions.

Inspire Trust with Website Content

Your website's message—what it says and how it says it—can persuade visitors to become customers. Regardless of the number of pages on your site or the type of content you put on them, consistency and accuracy are the cornerstones of crafting a trustworthy web message. A website rife with spelling and grammatical errors projects a business that lacks attention to detail in its products and services. A site that leaves out important details or critical information to help a customer do business with you says in effect, "We don't really care."

Your website visitors also may be looking for specific content that will reassure them and reinforce your dependability. Let's next look at some of the key items that you should consider including on your website to help build more trust between your site and your customers.

State Your Strength with Microcontent

In Chapter 5, I explained the importance of using microcontent to make your small site functional, informative, and—above all—useable. Because microcontent—elements like page titles, meta tags, and headlines—really directs a visitor's experience with your site, it can play a critical role in establishing your business's trustworthiness.

The Web has a certain timeless quality to it. Sites can be here today and gone tomorrow. (Or more commonly here today, forgotten tomorrow, but still here a year from tomorrow.) Websites also are not tied to a particular location. You can just as easily find a financial adviser or caterer the next time zone over as you can the next street over. That's why, when used as page title or callout headline on your home page, trust-building taglines or mottos that emphasize the length of time you've been in business and the markets that you've served can quickly answer questions visitors have about your business. Good examples include phrases like "Springfield's only film production rental business," "Serving Whoville since 1948," and "Serving Austin cyclists since 1999."

Be Consistent with Your Critical Content

Make sure that all of your online content is clear, consistent, and up-to-date. It's easy to forget or just lose track of a price or incentive you may have offered on an old web page. But you should assume that the contents of your website are subject to the same "truth in advertising" laws and restrictions as a newspaper or television ad. (And even if you're not legally bound, you should consider yourself ethically bound to honor the published contents of your website.) In Chapter 9, I'll provide small site update strategies that will help you avoid the problems of an out-of-date site.

Likewise, maintain consistency with your website design. Don't use your website as an excuse to be "creative" or "different." Inconsistency breeds distrust. Use the same colors and logos on your website as you do elsewhere in your business—for example, on signage, flyers, menus, and the like.

Provide Credible Visual Cues

The best way to do this is to include a photo of your physical location, a photo of yourself, or both. Such photos can snuff out doubts among visitors who may inherently question that you are who you say you are and you do what you say you do. Personal pictures are especially helpful for businesses offering personal services. A picture of your building or office offers the added benefit of assisting people coming to your location for the first time (see Figure 7.2). On the other hand, if you're running your business out of your spare bedroom, don't use unrelated clip art to represent your "office." The last thing you want to do is perpetuate a lie—even one that starts as a joke—on your website.

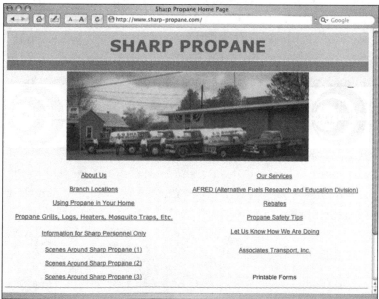

Figure 7.2
The picture of its brick-and-mortar operation on the Castle
Kitchens website (top) adds legitimacy to its online endeavors.
And while the Sharp Propane site (bottom) isn't necessarily the
paragon of great website design, it has one thing going for it: The
black-and-white location photo on its home page quickly conveys
the length of time the company has been in business at the same
location.

Other visual cues that can help establish your credibility include professional credentials—the logo of a professional association, accrediting body, or civic organization. If your business is a member in good standing for your local trade association or chamber of commerce, add the logo to your site. Even the proverbial "union label" makes sense for certain sites and audiences.

Credentials are like brands. We might take them for granted because we see them around a lot, but we all respond to them and recognize them. They also make us feel comfortable at an intuitive level and communicate a certain level of trust and quality control. A site that displays credentials well can better communicate to its visitors that it represents a legitimate business. Of course, it is also important to not go crazy with the credentials you display. A site or home page that looks like a race car with logos and certification labels plastered all over it can be a turnoff.

Create the Best Customer Service Page You Possibly Can

Web designers love to proclaim how important home pages are. After all, first impressions are everything, right? My thinking is that if website designers devoted even a quarter of the time they spend designing home pages to designing effective customer service pages instead, we would have many more happy website customers.

No matter how good your business is and how perfectly designed your website is, your customers will need help from time to time. They will need help finding information on your site, help matching products or services to their unique needs, help with ordering and shipping, help finding the contact information for your company, and possibly help when things go wrong.

Instead of spreading customer service information around various places on your site (on the home page, ordering page, product information page), consider creating a main customer service section and make sure that you have well-placed links to it from your home page and other key areas of your small site (see Figure 7.3). With this approach, a customer will always know where to go when they encounter a problem or have a question. This will greatly reduce the level of frustration that customers experience when they are trying to solve a pressing problem like trying to track down an order, ask a question, or return a product. Once you have a customer service section, you can

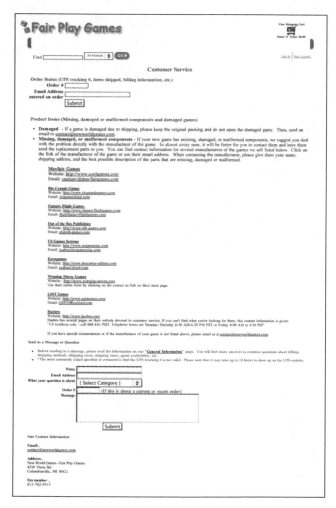

Figure 7.3
The customer service page for an online game retailer offers a plethora of options for handling customer questions and problems: online order tracking, instructions for handling missing or damaged orders, Web and email links for all the brands it carries, a contact form, and its physical address and phone number.

add pages to present important information that the customer will likely be looking for. For example, the site shown in Figure 7.4 details the customer service options that the company provides.

The customer service area is a good place to include the following information (or at least access to this information):

- Your complete contact information, including your hours of operation and an estimate of the time it will take you to respond to a customer query.

Figure 7.4
A furniture retailer's site outlines the important process of doing business with the site. This kind of information can really help set good expectations for the customer.

- Your policies about ordering, shipping, and returning products (if you offer products for sale).

- Your policies about any services that you offer as part of your business.

- Any information you can provide about your quality control efforts, your approach to ensuring customer satisfaction, and so on.

Customer service information like this can be easily presented in a FAQ format. If you take this approach, try to anticipate the types of questions that your customers will ask. Make sure that you state your policies as clearly as you can.

Don't Skimp on Important Shipping Information

If you sell (and ship) products, provide clear information about your shipping practices and policies (see Figure 7.5). For sites that sell products, this is some of the most important information that will be presented on your site. Your shipping information needs to be very clear, and you need to be very careful about the expectations that you set. Customers may purchase products from you based on what they understand as your shipping practices only to later find out that your

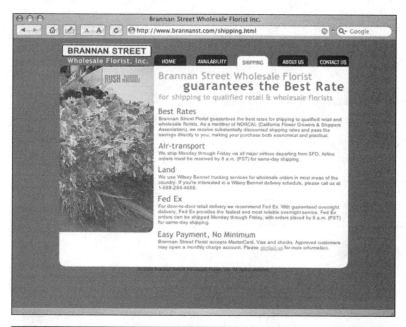

Figure 7.5
Fresh flowers and tuxedos have unique shipping requirements, and these online purveyors offer specific options and assurances on their shipping pages about how they get their goods to customers intact and on time.

policies are misleading or that you don't actually follow them. You should always make sure that you regularly review your shipping policies.

Always State Your Mission

Put a page (or just a paragraph) on your site that explains who you are and why you're in business. You can call it what you want—company history, mission statement, philosophy—but just do it and make it as accurate as you can. Don't overwhelm people with your life story; just give them enough to feel as if they know a little about you and will be satisfied doing business with you.

Don't put your business's mission statement in some forgotten corner of your site and then completely overwhelm it with links to "kickback" affiliate programs, unrelated partner sites, and little spinning dollar signs around the entrance to your online store. Things like this make your site visually cluttered, and they make an unambiguous statement about your site's real mission.

Make Your Privacy Policy Crystal Clear

If you request personal information from visitors to your website—and especially if you do any kind of e-commerce—you'll greatly improve your response rate if you disclose how you plan to use the information they give you with a privacy policy or a short one- or two-sentence disclaimer (see Figure 7.6). Writing a privacy policy can be a daunting task for a small site operator. For inspiration, take a look at the privacy policies for your bank, website hosting company, or competitors or consult with online privacy experts like VeriSign, TRUSTe, and the P3P Project of the World Wide Web Consortium. If writing your website's privacy policy never makes it to the top of your to-do list, at least offer your visitors a brief description of how you will and won't use the personal information they provide and a straightforward way to opt out of any future contact from your business.

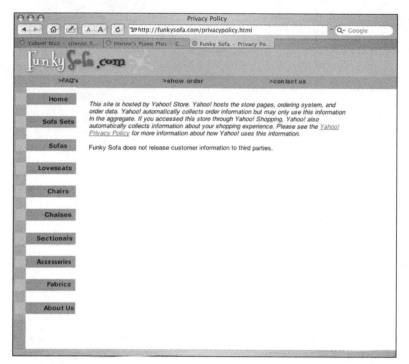

Figure 7.6
Funky Sofa, which uses Yahoo for its e-commerce, acknowledges
Yahoo's usage terms on its privacy policy page and adds a line of its
own about what it does with customer information.

Don't Leave Your Customers Guessing when Errors Occur

Use explanatory messages and automatic error pages when site features become unavailable or old pages are removed from your site (see
Figure 7.7). Web surfers are quick to assume a problem is their fault,
and repeated attempts to load a page can lead to frustration, then
dissatisfaction with—or worse, disinterest in—your business. If you go
to your industry's annual convention and can't update your weekly
specials page, post a virtual "gone fishing" sign with an explanation
and, more importantly, the date of the next scheduled update. An
error page, like a TV station test pattern, reassures visitors to your site
that the problem is yours, not theirs. Better yet, an error page can
guide those who see it to active pages on your site where they can find
what they are looking for.

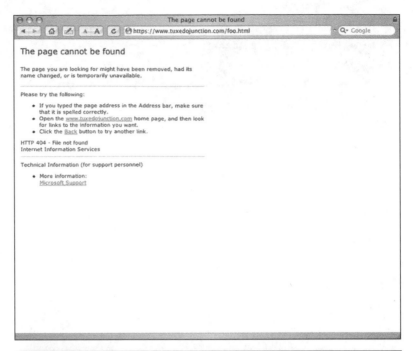

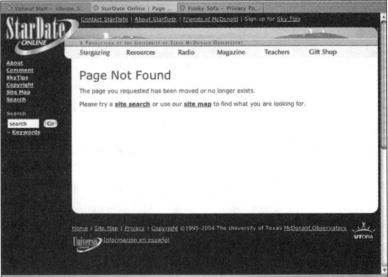

Figure 7.7
A web server's default error page (top) usually doesn't give visitors a meaningful reason why the page they tried to view isn't there. A useful error page (bottom) explains the problem to visitors in plain language and offers alternative ways to find what they're looking for. Often the solution is as simple as creating a customized error page (called error.html) based on your site's design template and uploading it to your web server.

Inspire Trust with Website Practices

If you see your website as nothing more than a one-to-many message-dispensing machine, you're not doing what it takes to build a trusting relationship between your business and your site visitors. Trust requires a dialog between you and your site visitors, and your website offers many ways to interact with them. Here are some good habits for running a successful small site.

Eliminate Errors

Make sure your site visitors never see an error page or misspelled word by testing, retesting, and proofreading your website religiously. (Do it every Sunday, if that helps.) Browse every page on your site regularly to check all the links and submit all the forms.

Respond Quickly

Surveys of major corporations have shown that many never respond to email sent via their website, so here's your chance to distinguish yourself from the big guys. People often write messages from websites as if no one will ever read them—it's a chance to vent or let off steam—so surprise them with a prompt and personal response.

If the volume of messages becomes too great, set up an auto-responder to let people know you received their email. The auto-response can even provide answers to common questions or a link back to key pages on your site, such as your frequently asked questions page. Even with an auto-responder in place, try to write a personal response whenever possible within two or three days.

Use Encryption

Spend the extra money (around $100 a year) to have your web hosting company purchase and install a Secure Sockets Layer (SSL) certificate for your domain in order to encrypt the browser-server connections and let people know that you have it. (The two primary certificate authorities—Thawte and VeriSign—both can provide you with a badge to display on your site.) It's an absolute requirement for transactions that require a credit card, and very reassuring for visitors asked to submit other personal or confidential information such as Social Security numbers, account numbers, or passwords. Don't ever ask people to email their credit card number to you. Those that do are likely providing fraudulent payment information and those that (wisely) refuse are not likely to return to your site.

Get Reviewed

Organizations like TRUSTe, the Better Business Bureau, and Gomez, among others, provide website performance, complaint handling, and privacy policy reviews, as well as dispute resolution, usually for a fee that varies depending on your business's annual sales. When its review is complete, you can display the organization's seal of approval on your website (see Figure 7.8). Consumer WebWatch (**consumerwebwatch.org**), an offshoot of *Consumer Reports* magazine, offers a complete list of website trust-building tools and resources, including information for website publishers who provide financial, health, or kids-specific content.

Figure 7.8
Badges like these go a long way toward proving that visitors won't get burned when doing business on a site.

Pursue and Resolve Disputes

You may not be the only one who has heard from the customer who thinks they were wronged when doing business with your website. In addition to the Better Business Bureau, which has been fielding and recording complaints about offline businesses since 1912, there are a number of other complaint clearinghouses that track Internet fraud, including the Internet Fraud Complaint Center (**www1.ifccfbi.gov**) and Consumer Sentinel (**www.consumer.gov/sentinel**). Your state's attorney general also may have information about your business that needs your attention. Invest the time to discover and settle disputes before they start having a negative impact on your business.

Encourage Visitors to Take Action

Even without the whizbang features that many mistakenly assume are necessary for a successful site, your small site can encourage visitors to interact with you and your business. With your visitors' attention focused on your business and trust established, your site visitors are ready to take action—which may mean making a purchase, requesting a sales call, submitting a survey in exchange for a coupon, or even providing you with valuable feedback about your site.

Be Consistent and Repeat Yourself

In Chapter 4, I explained the importance of maintaining consistency in the design and navigation of your small site. Consistency keeps visitors focused on your business, not on how your website works. Consistency evokes reliability and trust.

Consistency also plays a crucial role in emphasizing what you want visitors to your site to do. Highlight and repeat what you want your website visitors to do on every page on your site, whether it's to sign up for your mailing list, download a coupon, fill in a survey, or make a purchase or donation.

Ask the Right Questions to Determine If You're Getting Results

Regardless of what actions you want your site visitors to take, their responses will likely be submitted through a form. In Chapter 5, I covered the design and functional do's and don'ts of using forms on your site.

Forms also can help you track the effectiveness of your website and other marketing activities—if you ask the right questions and understand why people do or don't fill in forms on the Web.

Here are a few common reasons you might use a form on your website and reasons why your site visitors will take the time to fill it out:

- You want to solicit comments, questions, criticisms, and suggestions about your business—and gauge the ways people are finding your site. Your customers and potential customers have things they want to tell you, and many of them are going to the Web looking for a way to do it. A comment form—easily the most common type of form on the Web—is the perfect solution. After the form field for email address (which should be required so you can follow up or add them to your mailing list) and the text field for their message, ask them how they heard about your business. Use a pull-down menu of preset choices that lists the ways you're trying to get the word out about your site, such as Google, classified ads, the web address painted on the side of your business vehicle, or any of the other low-cost marketing strategies I outlined in Chapter 6. Change the choices as your marketing efforts change, and don't forget to ask if they're a first-time or repeat visitor, too.

- A survey or needs assessment form can help you build up a list of business prospects and find out more about your potential customers' needs in a way that doesn't tie up your time or phone line. Visitors who want a follow-up call or a discount on their first order will spend the time to give you their email address, phone number, and answers to short screening questions. Like the "how did you find us" question on your comment form, your screening questions should offer preset choices—this time from search-engine keyword phrases that you hope people have used to find your site. For example, a therapist who specializes in treating childhood trauma and eating disorders should ask potential patients about their interest in those specific services.

- A form can help you get feedback about your site itself and identify problem areas that your testing missed. In order to track down the problem, ask for the page address, the browser, and computer operating system your visitor was using and as much additional information about the problem as they can provide. You won't get this much detail even half the time, but when you do, it's a big help in keeping your site running smoothly.

- You don't need a full-blown shopping cart to generate new revenue from your site when a scaled-down order form can do the trick. Potential customers who know your business and have come to your website for one or two popular products will appreciate the simplicity of being able to order what they want quickly without the hassle of learning a new shopping cart system. (Remember, your site is not Amazon.com.) In a nutshell, an order form forgoes the page-to-page browsing and multistep checkout process of a shopping cart in favor of a one-page, one-step form that features a small product selection—a case of your award-winning salsa or the must-have gizmo that brought everyone to your site in the first place. With an order form, you can easily change your online product mix to offer what sells well, ships easily, and makes the most profit.

Forms Can Be the Undoing of Your Site

Forms stand between you and your anonymous website visitors. The process of putting names and faces to the people who visit your site and turning them into loyal customers hinges on whether your website succeeds in getting your site visitors to perform the tasks you're offering.

People will skip or give up on your website when the forms you present are too long, offer little or no advantage for filling them out, ask questions that are too personal, or simply don't work. When visitors to your site fail to take the action you desire, all the effort you've put into capturing their attention and establishing trust goes for naught.

Summary

In this chapter you learned how you can improve your small site's chance of success by inspiring trust in your visitors. Your website has to turn the tide of web surfer skepticism with content that reinforces your business's dependability. You learned which website management practices and habits will provide the evidence your visitors need to prove that there is a real business—and real people—behind your website. Trust is the key to creating the relationships that convert website visitors into customers.

GETTING WHAT YOU NEED FROM YOUR WEB DESIGNER

8

- Learn how to choose a designer who can help you create and design your small site.

- Learn how to keep costs down and ensure that your designer builds the site you want.

- Learn how to work with a designer to save time and money.

At the height of the dot-com boom a few years ago, one of David Letterman's running gags was to admit to his audience that he had taken up designing web pages in his spare time. The joke, of course, was that everyone and their dog was designing websites at the time. Many still are—people, that is; the dogs all cashed out at the top of the market.

As with the desktop publishing revolution of the mid-1980s, the results of the "democratization" of web design are mixed. Not all web designers are created equal. Not all web designers even call themselves web designers, or have the right skills and—more importantly—the right motives for building your small website.

In this chapter, you will learn why finding and working with the right web designer can make the difference between an unrefined or even amateur-looking site and a professional-looking one. I will dissect the various titles web designers go by so you can make an informed choice about the set of skills you need from someone who is building your website. Finally, you will learn the steps to take (and missteps to avoid) when working with a web designer to create a successful small site for your business.

Do You Really Need a Web Designer?

If you're like me—a do-it-yourself kind of person—you might be wondering if you really need a designer for your small site. After all, a small site is simple and doesn't require numerous or complex pages. You might be thinking that only large sites need designers and web teams to create and manage all of the web pages that they provide.

Many small site creators and small business owners will discover that they can do all or most of the work on their own. But not all of you will have the time, interest, or technical or design experience to create what you need. In such a case, employing the services of a web designer for your small site is a smart idea.

The right web designer can help you make your site look good by ensuring that it has just the right professional design polish. Just think about all of the print brochures you see that are produced by do-it-yourself business owners who are trying to save a few dollars. Often, they miss the boat in the design category and sometimes they can look downright cheesy. When producing business communications like this—and your website certainly is one—it's never a good idea to cut corners or put your business's image at risk. You've certainly heard that people judge you by the way that you look, and when it comes to your business, people do their judging with their dollars.

If you are having difficulty deciding if you really need a web designer to help you create you site, here are some issues to consider:

- **Designers can help you get the best perspective**. The right designer, especially one with small site design experience, can help you get focused on what should be incorporated into your site. Doing everything yourself makes it difficult to stand back and get the right perspective. An objective designer can take all of the elements that you think should be included on your site and help you prioritize the ones that are important and leave out the ones that are not needed.

- **Designers can help you save time and money**. An experienced web designer knows all of the tricks for getting things done quickly and saving time and money. If you are trying to create your own website for the first time, you can waste a lot of time on false starts or trying to adapt all your existing materials for the Web, not to mention fixing portions of your website that turn out differently than you really want, all of which may cause you to have to redesign your site.

- **Designers can help you properly promote your company image**. Designers can ensure that you promote your company identity and logo online. I often see businesses do a good job of promoting their image offline only to set up their own websites and undermine their efforts by, for example, changing the shape or color of their logo, changing their marketing slogans, and using "hip" typefaces that differ from what they typically use, in effect taking a simple and friendly business and turning it into an online monster. A good designer can serve as a sort of company "identity cop" and make sure that you stay true to the image that you've worked hard to create for your business.

- **The right designer can help you create a site that can be readily maintained**. As you've learned in this book, *creating* a website is only half of the battle. Websites are dynamic by nature and they require regular updates and fine-tuning to stay successful. Experienced web designers can help you create templates and other devices to help you better automate the process of keeping your site up-to-date. By working with a designer, you might spend a little more money up front but you could really save a lot of time and money in the long run. In this respect, working with a designer early on in the process can be a smart investment.

- **Designers can help you expand your design sense.** Because your time is limited, you can explore only a certain number of websites to get design ideas. You might have already convinced yourself that your site should look a certain way because you don't have time to explore more options. Good designers eat and breathe websites, and they are always on the lookout for better ways to communicate ideas and make sites more interactive and dynamic.

Choose a Web Designer Who Meets Your Needs

As you've been learning in this book, creating a small website takes a certain mindset. Many designers have a lot of experience designing large sites that provide lots of bells and whistles for their clients. A designer who has experience creating large sites may work for you, but you'll need to make sure that they can produce what you actually need. The most important thing that you can do is search out talented designers who have successfully built small sites.

You might find the small-site expert you're looking for by seeking a recommendation from your Internet service provider or web hosting company. A colleague, or even a competitor, may know of a web designer who specializes in creating sites for your type of business (see Figure 8.1). Some savvy web designers even put their company name in the fine print at the bottom of sites they designed, like a dealership logo on the back of a new car. If you find a site you like, scroll down to the bottom of the page to see if the designer has signed their work or just email the business owner to ask who designed the site.

Take the time you need to talk "philosophy" with the designers you interview. If you need to, give them a copy of this book and make sure that they understand the real value of designing a small site.

Figure 8.1
Some web design companies offer price-point packages or specialize in certain types of business websites.

Assessing Your Real Needs

Your role in the relationship you will have with your web designer is to keep the project—your website—focused on the needs and goals of your business rather than those of your designer. If you've read the previous seven chapters, you know that a successful small site focuses on how your business and your website can benefit your customers. With a small, successful site, you can do more with less and avoid the trappings of over-design that lead to an unmanageable, and unusable site.

You want a site that gets your message across, a site that is easy to update and maintain (a topic we'll revisit in Chapter 9), and a site that fits your business. Ideally, your web designer will be someone who understands your goals and, better yet, your business or industry.

Who's Who: A Web Designer by Any Other Name

By far the most common title for someone who builds websites is *web designer*. Often a person with a background in art or graphic design, a web designer usually focuses on the "front end" of websites—the colors, graphics, and layout that people see when your site loads in their browser.

Web designers should have a thorough knowledge of Hypertext Markup Language (HTML) and the use of web authoring software such as Macromedia Dreamweaver, Adobe GoLive, and Microsoft FrontPage. A web designer might also be proficient in Flash animation and using JavaScript to create dynamic HTML, such as navigation rollover effects.

A web designer may not know how to configure your web server or write complicated server-side scripts in languages such as ASP, PHP, or Perl. As artists, web designers often shun the technical side of website building.

You should be on the lookout for a web designer with a background in another visual medium, such as four-color printing or video production. The Web shares traits with both the print and broadcast media worlds, so a web designer with a knowledge of the various disciplines should be able to design a site that respects and observes both the similarities and the differences.

A web designer who meets these criteria can be an ideal choice, especially if they can assist you with your other design needs, such as business cards, brochures, flyers, and menus.

A *web developer* usually offers more programming or technical know-how than a web designer. They may even have better design skills than you do but prefer to focus on the functionality, or "back end," of website building: forms, scripting, databases, and browser-server interaction.

Web developers should be fluent in a variety of server technologies and scripting languages and have a working knowledge of the "do's and don'ts" of HTML. Knowledge of e-commerce tools, such as shopping cart software and credit card merchant account systems, is a plus, especially if you plan to move into online sales.

Lacking the strong design sensibilities of a web designer, your typical web developer may not be able to produce a "beautiful" website. But beauty is in the eye of the beholder, and for many developers, highly functional websites have an elegant beauty.

An experienced web developer may have a college degree in computer science or a third-party certification for one or more of the technologies they purport to know.

Hire a web developer if you want your website to stress function over form—or if you're willing to coordinate the efforts of both a nontechnical designer and a developer to create a site that excels at both form and function.

Other Names to Know

In your search for someone to build your site, you may encounter other job titles like web producer, webmaster, information architect, or even user interface designer. A *web producer* offers a combination of design and programming skills, though they may not be a master of either. Web producers also can work with designers and developers to "put it all together" and remain "on call" as your site changes and grows.

Webmaster is a term coined in the earliest days of the Web. A webmaster might be someone who oversees all facets of a website's operation in a small enterprise. In a large business, the webmaster usually deals specifically with keeping a website's hardware and software tuned up and running at all times.

Information architect is a fancy term for hypertext librarian. They specialize in how navigation and content can be organized, searched, and archived in a hypertext environment to maximize the user experience. *User interface designers* focus on the front-end experience across a variety of interactive interfaces, from kiosks to PDAs to websites. User interface designers may not be proficient with actual HTML code, but they know what works and what doesn't in an interactive or online experience. Hiring an information architect or user interface designer is probably more in terms of expertise—not to mention expense—than you need for your small site.

Hiring the Right Person for Your Small Site

Choosing someone to build your website gives new meaning to the phrase "comparing apples and oranges." Skills and specializations have more variety than a Shoney's salad bar. Keep in mind that many people in the web-building profession portray themselves according to one of the titles I've just described but have skills from more than one discipline. (For the rest of this chapter, I'll use the title *web designer* to refer to all manner of website builders.)

Also remember the old adage that if your only tool is a hammer, every problem looks like a nail. Website builders tend to gravitate toward what they know, so keep that in mind when choosing one to work on your site. That goes for the built-in site-builder tools available with many web hosting plans, too. The one-size-fits-all approach can leave your site looking sloppy.

Judge your prospective web designers by their websites—both their own and the ones they've recently completed. Here are some questions you should consider when evaluating sites that have been created by a designer you are considering:

- Do the sites have good focus and not try to do too much?

- Are the sites easy to use?

- Can you easily find important information such as customer service information, contact information, and so on?

- Do the sites present text that is scannable, navigation that is clear and intuitive, and graphics that are lightweight and appropriate for the business they represent?

- Do the sites really show off the businesses they are designed for, and do they make you want to do business with them?

- Did the designer avoid the trappings of bloated and hard to use sites—slow-loading Flash graphics, cumbersome navigation, disorganization?

- Do the sites provide meaningful feedback when something goes wrong?

- Are the business owners for the sites happy with them and do they feel they really help complement and promote their businesses? (Always check references.)

Look for common themes or practices. If every site they've created features a giant splash screen, you can bet that an unnecessary splash page will be part of that designer's vision for your site as well.

Even if every site in a designer's portfolio looks more or less the same, if they meet your criteria for what your site should be and adhere to the small-site standards laid out in this book, you're probably on the right track. But just as you would for someone you want to remodel your kitchen or print your business cards, get at least a couple of bids for your project and talk to some of a prospective web designer's past clients to get a feel for their work ethic, responsiveness, and attention to detail.

Don't forget that web designers are business people too. They want to satisfy their customers, just like you. Word-of-mouth marketing for a job well done can lead to referrals for more work. They also want respect for their expertise, not a client who will second-guess their work. And, of course, web designers want to be fairly compensated.

Know What Things Cost

So that brings up the issue of what web designers charge: Some charge per page, others per project, and others by the hour.

For example, a 10-page site might cost anywhere from $500 to $1500. Website setup and a single-page site might cost you $200 to $500. (Wal-Mart-owned Sam's Club recently launched a new service for its small-business customers: $5 a month for a website and custom design services starting at $99.) A snazzy home page graphic might cost you another couple hundred bucks. Hourly rates can vary from $25 for a recent college grad to $150 and up for a full-service web design agency.

Where you decide to spend your website building dollars depends on what you want to do with your site. For a tiny starter site of two or three pages that rarely needs to be updated, you might opt for a web designer with a reputation for creating clean, attractive, usable sites with stand-out visual impact. For slightly larger sites that will have an ongoing need for updates and new pages, you might forgo the upscale eye candy in favor of a web designer with experience, a track record for reliability, and an hourly rate that won't break the bank.

Also, learn the "buzz words." Find out what technologies will save you money and which ones may end up costing you. A web designer committed to building efficient, usable sites with technologies like Cascading Style Sheets (CSS) and World Wide Web Consortium (W3C) accessibility standards has your website's best interests in mind, whereas one who emphasizes their work in Flash, Java, or ASP.NET may want to push your site in a direction with high payoff for him but little benefit for you.

Getting Started and Working with a Designer

You've now learned why you might need a designer for your small site and how you should go about hiring one. Let's now look at how you can work with a designer to get the best results. My goal here is to show you how to get great results and save time and money.

Building a website requires a number of steps, including the registration of one or more new domains and selecting and signing up for a web hosting account as well as the actual design, production, and maintenance of the site itself. In this section, we'll focus on the actual design and production stage. This will give you a good idea of the process that you'll likely go through with a designer as you get your site built. Of course, the specifics of designing a site will vary from site to site and from business to business. There are, however, some general approaches that we can discuss that are common to designing most small sites.

Magic or Method?

If you're starting from scratch, you may be tempted to just hand over all your materials—logo, graphics, photos, and text—to your web designer and tell them to "work their magic." This might seem like a good approach because it frees you from having to make too many decisions or get too involved, but you'll probably be disappointed by the results you get. Remember, the designer is not the publisher of your site; you are. Unless you have worked with your designer before and they can read your mind, you'll likely end up with a site that pleases your designer but is disappointing to you. After all, no one knows your business better than you do, and the more you communicate your needs and ideas, the better your chances will be of achieving success.

The more methodical process for working with a designer would be to follow the steps, or "milestones," I've outlined here:

1. **Meet to discuss scope.** When you've chosen the web designer you want to work with, arrange a meeting—preferably sans computers—to get to know each other and talk about your proposed site. Many people—and especially web designers—like to brainstorm visually, so be prepared to sketch out some ideas on paper and bring a list of sites that you'd like to emulate. Keep in mind when choosing sites for design inspiration that even the best web designers can't make your small boutique's website look like Bananarepublic.com—at least not without a significant investment from you for the creation of the photos, graphics, and marketing copy that large sites need to sustain a visitor's interest.

In your first meeting with your web designer, be sure to cover critical topics such as the following:

- What will the site's focus be?

- How many pages do you expect the site to be?

- What kind of original materials do you have to work with? (You might consider putting together a content inventory for your designer to outline the copy, images, and other assets you want to include on the site.)

- Are there any upcoming events (a trade show or sale) that will influence when the site needs to be done?

- How will the site need to grow or change in the first year or two?

- Who will be in charge of certain tasks such as reformatting or rewriting content for the site or making updates?

- Don't be shy about stating your expectations—even your budget—so your web designer has a good idea of your intended scope for the site and what's realistic given the resources you have available for it.

2. **Start with a design concept.** Your designer can create one or more design concepts for your site using the logo and other materials you provide. A static mock-up lacks the clickable interactivity of an HTML-based web page, but it will give you a sense for how the pages will look and the opportunity to suggest changes. To prepare

for this step, make sure that you gather all of the important images that help define your business logo treatments, the text fonts you use, and so on. Make sure that you communicate to your designer the actual colors and other specific formats that you use with your business communications.

3. **Build working templates.** Your designer can now take the mock-up that you both agree on and create one or more HTML templates. These templates will be master web pages containing the common elements that will be on all (or most) of the pages on your site. Using a template ensures that the pages maintain a consistent look throughout your site.

4. **Test out your pages.** Your designer can upload the finished web pages to a special area of their website where you can preview the work. If they (or you) want the pages to appear on your site as they're completed, you'll have to give your designer FTP access to your web server.

   Before your site is ready for public consumption (or "launched"), you'll want to spend some time testing (which we'll come back to in a moment) and registering it with search engines (which we discussed in Chapter 6).

Working in Phases

If the term *work in progress* had a poster child, most sites on the Web would qualify. That's not necessarily a bad thing.

Building a small, simple site often involves setting priorities and making choices about what to do first and what can wait until later. There's nothing wrong with letting your site evolve over time, especially if your budget, or business model, or the time you have available dictates an incremental approach.

Know When to Cut Corners and When to Plan for Growth

Beware of cutting corners in the extreme. Don't push for the quick and simple way of doing something on your site the first time to save time and money only to have to step back to square one when the time comes to upgrade. In the parlance of computer professionals, it's called *scalability*—can your website grow with your business.

For example, a contact page with two or three names and email addresses may serve your needs on day one. When the contact list grows beyond about a dozen addresses, a form that forwards your visitors' messages to the desired address becomes the better way to handle emails from your website. A contact form for just two or three addresses can easily grow to accommodate more addresses, while the simple list—cheaper at first—quickly becomes impractical as your site grows (see Figure 8.2).

Dealing with Problems: Yours, Mine, and Ours

Don't let the process of building your website devolve from point-and-click to pointing fingers. Problems involved in getting a website from concept to completion often pit the "naïve, misinformed" client (how your web designer will see you) against the "arrogant, unresponsive" designer (how you see them).

Here are a few suggestions for making sure that never happens.

Take Time to Test

Like flossing and eating your broccoli, testing your web designer's work is a necessary evil of creating a website. Few people enjoy the work. Those that do—quality assurance engineers, who are the proofreaders of large sites—can be a strange breed, and your web designer, while possibly strange in many ways, probably doesn't like to do it either. But everyone needs an editor. Inherent to the process of creating something is a blind spot to its faults.

Give your site a test drive. Try it out on more than one computer: your home computer, your office computer, the computer at the public library. Check every link and submit every form. Ask a couple of friends or coworkers to help out.

Don't assume that a problem with the site is your fault. And don't assume that something looks wrong just because you don't know what you're doing. You're much better off uncovering problems while your designer is still in your employ than six months later.

If you plan on being active with your site once it is created by the designer, make sure that you let your designer know up front that you plan to work with the templates and other files that they create for you. You might ask your designer to spend some time with you to show you how the templates work. You could even ask your designer to create a template-based sample page that includes a palette of dummy page elements such as headlines, subheads, information boxes, and download icons and other images that you can copy and paste into your actual web pages.

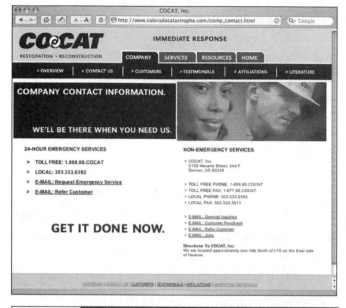

Figure 8.2

A list of email addresses on the top site lets visitors choose a destination for their comment. A pull-down menu on another site's contact form (bottom) offers more flexibility in adding new destinations for emails that originate from your website.

Agree on a Standard of Completion

Your website may never be "done," but you and your designer should agree on when the work they're doing for you is complete. You may wish to have all the files uploaded to your web server and tested in place before handing over the final payment. Your web designer may be uncomfortable turning over the fruits of their labor before being fully compensated. To avoid a stalemate, plan to do the uploading, testing, training, and paying in a one- or two-hour session at your office, your designer's office, or a neutral location with Internet access like Starbucks.

Don't Let Your Web Designer Hold You Hostage

Control of your website is a powerful responsibility to entrust to someone. But with the complexity of the Web, many people want to turn over the helm to an expert.

For a small business owner, the practice is tantamount to leaving the keys to your business with your leasing agent and having to call them to unlock the door every time you want to go to work. Too often, site owners find themselves captive to their hired experts, who've long since moved on to other projects—or professions.

Separation of Powers

Exert some control over the process by keeping the hosting and domain name registration accounts separate from web design services. Don't let your web designer own your domain or host your site. If you ever find yourself in a dispute over their work, you won't have much influence to sway the outcome in your favor.

Companies that specialize in web hosting will usually register a domain name on your behalf when you sign up for one of their hosting plans. And unlike your web designer, who doesn't want to know that your site is down at six in the morning, all the reputable hosting companies guarantee near-100-percent uptime, notify you of planned downtime, and provide 24-hour technical support by email, phone, or even live web page chat sessions.

Take Delivery on Deliverables

A website can be a rather abstract, ephemeral creature—just a pile of bytes, here today, gone tomorrow. But real work does go into creating a website, and as the site's owner, you should make sure you get something that proves the work was done.

Require your web designer to provide you with a CD of the website files when the work is done—the original, high-resolution graphics files as well as optimized images and web page code that they upload to your web server. If you ever need to have work done on your site by someone else—or have to revert to the original version of a page—you'll be able to do so easily.

Get It in Writing

Before your web designer cashes your last check, make sure you get all the pertinent information about the site from in writing. Require a one-page cheat sheet that includes all the necessary passwords, file locations, tech support phone numbers, explanations for why something was done in a certain way, and tips on updating the site yourself.

Building the Foundation

After sifting through all the design portfolios and technology acronyms to choose the web designer with the right combination of skills, experience, and price, you may still find yourself proselytizing the Small Site philosophy to a web designer who wants to do more with your site than you do. Certainly some will relish the challenge of building small. Others just want to do another site like the last 15 they've done—after all, there's safety in numbers.

Keep your goal of a small, simple site focused on your customers' needs foremost in the minds of everyone who works on your site. Stick to your guns in advocating the Small Site method.

Summary

In this chapter, you learned how to choose and work with the right web designer. You saw why working with a web designer can be well worth the expense. You also saw why—given the variety of skills and experience that web designers bring to their work—it's important to choose wisely. Hiring and collaborating with the right web designer is your first and best chance to build a small, successful site for your business.

KEEPING YOUR SMALL SITE UP-TO-DATE

9

- Learn about the benefits of having a site that is easy to update.

- Learn what you need to know to set up an easy-to-maintain site.

- Learn what you need to do to keep your site up-to-date.

A site that never gets updated won't be a successful site. The most popular sites on the web—news sites, weblogs, and auction sites, to name a few—draw repeat visitors (many of whom visit several times a day) hoping for the latest headline, blog entry, or price change.

You won't likely match the update frequency of these high-traffic sites—you have a business to run, after all—but there's a lesson to be learned from the relationship these sites have with their most fervent fans: fresh content on your website helps you build an audience of repeat visitors. And repeat visitors to a small site are the best candidates to become customers. If you want success from your small site, neglecting to update it is no different than printing a new flyer and forgetting to mail it.

In this chapter, we'll discuss the benefits of updating your site, what to update, and how you can make regular updates without the process taking over your life (at the expense of your business), cluttering your home page and other critical pages, or causing your site to slide off into bloatland. We'll review strategies for designing and organizing your site for updates. Finally, we'll identify some specific advanced methods and technologies that you can use to automate your site updates—or, at the very least, keep it painless and under your control.

Benefits of Updating

Few sites begin life on the web with no plans by their owners to change them, update them, or keep them fresh. If God had wanted websites to remain static, Tim Berners-Lee would have built the first webpage with a chisel and stone tablet, not a modified text editor, a mouse, and an internet connection. Websites are dynamic works-in-progress not historical plaques or tombstones.

The irony of the web is that with a bit of technical know-how and a few mouse clicks, you can publish new information about your business that can be read almost instantly by millions of people all over the world. Yet those seemingly modest hurdles lead far too many site owners to stumble, or never make it out of the starting blocks. I'm here to show you how to keep your footing when making regular site updates with techniques that will put your site head and shoulders above other small sites on the web.

Some of the major benefits of updating your site on a regular basis include:

* **Regular updates reinforce the relationships you want to build with site visitors and customers.** Fresh information on your site conditions people to expect something new when they visit, and that keeps them coming back for more. Even if they don't see something new on your site, the fact that they've returned creates an opportunity for them to notice something old, but of new-found importance to them (see Figure 9.1). Ignoring for a moment what your update might say, putting something new on your site strengthens the perception in your visitors' minds that your business is an active, going concern with real ways of benefiting them.

* **Updating your site helps you keep focused on your business.** Adding new information to your site keeps the integrity of your site (and your business) foremost in your mind and can easily be incorporated into your regimen of regularly browsing and testing the various components of your site. (Testing, which we covered in Chapter 8, is a critical factor in maintaining a useful and successful site.)

Figure 9.1
Devoting a corner of your home page to updates keeps new and repeat visitors informed about what's going on with your business. As this site shows, it is very important to make your site updates very visible so that your visitors don't have to search for them.

* **Identifying ways to update your site allows you to improve the design and functionality of your site.** The update process will help you build up a stockpile of ideas that you can use for brainstorming new updates or even rerunning old ones when you run out of ideas for a new update.

* **Keeping your site up-to-date gets easier over time.** While the prospect of committing to a schedule of regular site updates may seem daunting at first, it is a process that builds momentum and feeds itself over time. They say the first year of a marriage is the hardest. And though your lack of fidelity to updating your site—be it weekly, quarterly, or just occasionally—won't land you in divorce court, the first year updating your website will present the biggest challenge. But the effort will pay off.

How Often Should You Update Your Site?

Now that the benefits of updating your site on a regular basis are firmly planted in your mind (if not your daily schedule), let's turn to the question of how often to update. To be certain, something is better than nothing. But in keeping with the small site philosophy to do more with less because more is not necessarily better and striving for daily updates to a small site won't necessarily yield commensurate amounts of website success. In fact, that's a good way to tilt the balance of business benefit you get from your site into the red and tread upon the wasteland of bloat.

A good starter strategy is to plan for a few updates in the first year, timed to coincide with other marketing or merchandising efforts. For example, if you mail a coupon in a direct-mail card pack with offers from other local businesses, set yourself apart by offering a downloadable version of the coupon for visitors to your site (see Figure 9.2). If you make a habit of always buying space in an annual advertising supplement published by a local publication, reiterate your offer on your website.

Look for ways to peg your updates to seasonal sales patterns or new product shipments or annual events. Review your books for times when business peaks, and pique interest in your website with timely promos to match: florists at Valentine's Day, taxicab and livery service providers during the end-of-year holidays, safety equipment distributors during National Fire Prevention Week, and so on.

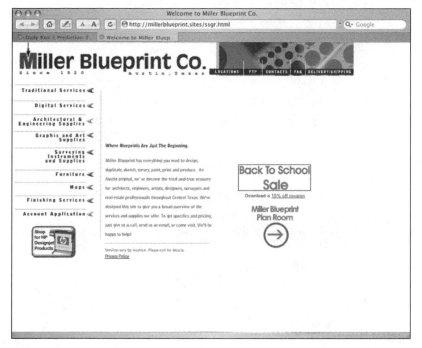

Figure 9.2
The online component for this art-supply store back-to-school sale lets customers who didn't get the printed flyer download a coupon from the home page.

TIP: As you do the work to create a new site or substantially change an existing site, I strongly encourage you to create an "update" calendar right from the start. Instead of trying to design everything into your new site launch, hold back some of the elements and plan them out for later in the year. You might even do some of the design work upfront so that you'll be ready to put up your updates later in the year. This planning approach can help you ensure that you put up updates in a timely manner and keep your site dynamic and fresh.

Developing a Realistic Approach and Schedule

Making occasional site updates that complement your existing and ongoing business efforts is the most realistic approach if you're new to web publishing or have just the bare minimum of time to commit to your site. Here are some specific tips that I can give you to help you develop a realistic approach and schedule for updating your small site:

- **Create an editorial calendar.** Look back over your calendars and appointment books for the past two or three years to generate a handful of ideas, and compile your best ideas on an editorial calendar that you can refer back to when you're stumped for new update ideas in the future.

- **Create a schedule you can live with**. Upgrading your update schedule to once a month, once a week, or even more often than that requires strict adherence to a schedule. Promising and failing to deliver is a worse sin in your visitors' eyes than never making the promise in the first place (see Figure 9.3). It's reminiscent of the old copy editor's rule to never call something the "First Annual" anything since it only becomes an annual event when you do it a second time a year after the first.

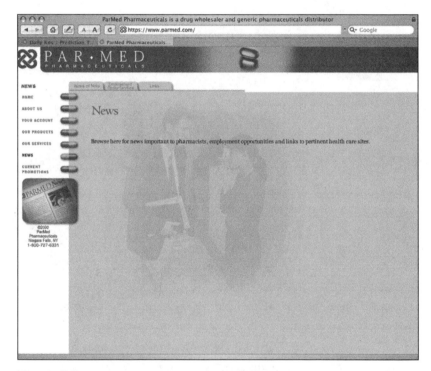

Figure 9.3
When "what's new" isn't: When you design a site with a news page, you should put something on it.

- **Don't get too ambitious with your updates**. Committing to a stricter schedule offers the potential of a higher payoff, as people make checking your site part of their regular web-surfing routine. But you run the risk of making your website your full-time job. And that risk can be even higher if you haven't already proven your reliability with regular, less-frequent updates.

- **Don't update your site too much and let bloat set in**. The options for serious small site updaters also present the risk of running your site into bloat territory. The need to ride herd over an ever-increasing universe of pages, downloads, or even forum postings can tax the time and budget of even the most dedicated site builder.

- **Consider using supplements to your web site to communicate updated information**. One safe alternative is a monthly or quarterly newsletter. If you're collecting email addresses, use them to direct people to a regularly updated newsletter page on your site (see Figure 9.4). Other options for frequent updates may require

Figure 9.4
The publication schedule for the first online newsletter seems a bit erratic, but it's presence on the company's websites is commendable nonetheless. The second newsletter is a quarterly.

THE LEAST YOU NEED TO KNOW TO UPDATE YOUR OWN SITE

Even if you're not an HTML code warrior, you can still make simple changes to your site with a text editor and a program for uploading new files to your webserver. Here are a few simple steps you can follow:

1. Have your web designer set up the page or pages you want to update with generic placeholders for the pieces of the page you want to update. Your highlighted message can be saved on your server as "promo_message.txt" and your promo image as "promo_image.jpg."

2. When the time comes to make an update, just upload a new file with the same name to replace the old. Since the placeholder code on the page doesn't change, the server will replace the old message or image with the new one, and *voila*, your page is updated.

Here's how all of this works in a nutshell:

- You have to connect to your webserver over the Internet to make a change to your website. File transfer protocol (FTP, see sidebar for more information) is the most common method, though better site-hosting plans come with online tools you can use to edit pages and upload files to your site.

- Webpages are written in hypertext markup language (HTML) a (mostly) human-readable type of computer code. An HTML file is a container for other files—stylesheets, scripts, images, include files, embedded movies—that are delivered in a batch from the server and compiled on the page by the browser.

- WYSIWYG webpage editors (such has Dreamweaver or FrontPage) hide a lot of the code, but will let you see it if you want to. Many experienced web designers started creating websites before graphical webpage editors matured, and can create and edit webpages with nothing more than a text editing program.

- Elements to be displayed on a webpage usually have to be enclosed in opening and closing tags to display correctly. For example, <html></html> tags start and end a webpage file; <body> and </body> tags delineate the part that the browser displays; <p> and </p> enclose a block of text to be displayed as a paragraph.

you to allow your visitors to become content creators on your site (through online forum postings or bulletin boards), which can require additional site complexity that can quickly take you beyond the realm of a small, simple site.

What You Should and Shouldn't Update

So let's assume that you've decided to commit yourself to an update plan such as making four updates a year to your website—one a quarter. Regular updates can excite and engage your visitors but should not surprise them when done right. Do it wrong and you'll leave your visitors shaking their heads in frustration as they wonder "Where did such-and-such go?" or "Is this the right site?" It all depends on what you choose to update.

Good updates are incremental improvements that extend or build upon the message or story you're trying to tell with your site. Adverse updates work against your site's success by derailing the relationships you want to foster with visitors through proper updates. Updating your website should become a habit but not an addiction.

For example, changing a highlighted message on you home page or replacing a featured product image won't shock your regular visitors. But avoid the temptation to change your site's color scheme (blue for winter, green for spring) or main navigation choices when the time comes to update.

Updating your site does not mean redesigning it—no matter how nicely your web designer asks. The last thing you want to do is make your visitors think they've come to the wrong site (I thought this site was blue!) or figure out (again) how you've reorganized your site since their last visit. In general, people don't always respond well to change unless the change is incremental.

Designing and Organizing Your Site for Updates

Establishing an update schedule, maintaining style guidelines and written documentation describing how to update your site, keeping like files together, and moving or deleting old pages are all part of a healthy plan for managing a successful small site. Together, they will make updates easier and keep your home page and other critical pages on your site clutter free.

Technology can help, but only so much. A successful site maintenance strategy requires that you develop good habits, routines, and procedures for building and updating your site before you think about the high-tech tools and automation techniques that fall under the term "content management" or "site management." Software can remind you when it's time to update your site (if you tell it to), but unfortunately, there's no program that will write the update for you. You have to do that yourself.

Many web builders think a high-tech content management system will be the magic bullet for stale, disorganized sites, but more often than not, a content management system adds to the confusion because of its steep learning curve, one-size-fits all approach, and expensive customization costs. Site management is really more about having a bit of editorial sensibility about your website. Remember that a website is a publication, after all and not just a technology gizmo.

Let's now look at some low-tech content management techniques that you can use to help you keep your website in order instead of relying on an overly complicated content management system. These techniques are all designed to save your time and money.

Document Your Workflow

If everything goes according to the small-site plan, your site will be up and running and you'll be following your update schedule and making changes to the site with ease. But before long, you'll wonder what you featured or updated on your site four months ago last Wednesday. Or you'll be on vacation or sick or trapped under something heavy when an important site update has to be made.

My small-site solution: Keep a three-ring binder of instructions and update guidelines so someone else can update your site in your absence. (In Chapter 9, I suggested making documentation a deliverable your web designer must provide before getting his last check.) Keep a record of site updates in the binder, too. Print out each webpage after a change, mark it with the date, and keep it for future reference. Pen-and-paper records have an advantage for a small business with a small website. They're inexpensive to create and maintain and everyone can use them without needing a password or training.

- Paragraphs in HTML automatically get an extra line of space below the last line of text—unless that default setting has been modified with a stylesheet.

- Most browsers can reliably display only JPEG, GIF and PNG image formats, so other image types such as PICTs, TIFFs, or bitmaps need to converted to one of those three formats before being placed on a webpage.

- Multiple spaces in your HTML code will be displayed as one space in the actual web page—unless you use code to specify additional "non-breaking spaces" in your code ( ). So if you use spaces to simulate a hanging indent in your Word documents, the indent will be lost when you paste into a webpage.

- Special characters like curly quotes ("), curly apostrophes ('), bullets (•), and long dashes (—) that look so classy in printed documents don't always render correctly in every browser unless they are encoded. Your webpage editor may be configured to do this automatically, but you'll want to check the settings to be sure. A good book about HTML should have a table of special characters and their corresponding HTML codes.

- Likewise, spaces in your webpage file names and server directory names can trip up some browsers, or at the very least render your webpage address with ugly "%20" in place of the spaces.

There's a technical side to keeping your site organized and manageable, too. Web servers have a tendency to become like the "Roach Motel" from that old TV commercial—files go in, but they don't come out. You can exterminate this bug before your site becomes infested by establishing some good site maintenance habits that help you keep the files you want and delete the ones you don't. (For the perpetually disorganized—and the rest of you, too—I highly recommend using a web authoring program such as Dreamweaver or GoLive to assist you with keeping similar website files together and archiving old pages.)

Organizing and Archiving Files

When you first start your small site, you may only have a handful of files—a home page, a contact page, maybe a few images, and a stylesheet. The easy way to organize your files is to have no organization, to save all your files at the top level of the webserver (called the "root") with no subfolders (or "directories"). But if you have more than a handful of files, or plan to add more through updates and measured site growth, then the "no-plan" organization plan will leave your site hard to manage.

Instead, start your site off with a structure that separates the files on your website by their type (image, webpage, and so on) and purpose (download, animation, script, and so on). If you have several webpages on your site (or plan to have several), create folders on your webserver that mirror your site navigation. In other words, save all your newsletters in a folder called "newsletters" and your product pages in a folder called "products." Separating your files into folders on your webserver helps you find just the file you need to update, and makes it harder to delete the picture of your catalog (catalog.jpg), when you meant to delete the downloadable version (catalog.pdf), which was out of date. Keeping JPEGs and PDFs in their own folders thwarts this mistake.

Thanks to the Internet Archive and Google caching, web pages live long after you've forgotten about them. Nonetheless, the day will come when you'll want (or need) to remove old files from your site. An informative error page (usually error.html, but consult your web host to be sure) can guide your site visitors to the new page that has replaced the one that turned up missing. If you move a page rather than delete it, you can put a redirect tag on the old page to forward visitors automatically to the new page.

Automate Site Updates

Finding a way to speed up tedious tasks is one of the main reasons computers were invented. Computers can also alleviate the drudgery of making website updates, but few of the best methods are appropriate for the novice site builder. If you're unnerved by the sight of source code, consider yourself warned or advised to find someone more knowledgeable to help you out.

Though not technically a website update technique, one fairly easy way to automate the way your site provides information to visitors is through an email auto-responder. When a visitor sends an email or submits a form on your site to an address that you've chosen, your server responds with a message sent to their in-box. The message can contain answers to frequently asked questions, your upcoming performance schedule, or other late-breaking news. Most respectable hosting companies provide a web-interface for adding and updating auto-responders, which makes them an appealing alternative for those who don't want to mess around with updating actual webpages.

Now we venture into nerd territory. Using javascript to rotate or randomize text or images on your home page offers a benefit to you and your visitors: You can copy a handful of messages or product images into the script all at once, making the need to update a little less frequent, and your visitor sees a new image or message every time she visits your site. A randomizer is great way to present testimonials from loyal customers; a script that rotates images can quickly cycle through a sampling of your product offerings. To find a javascript to use on your site, Google "javascript randomize" or search the third-party extensions of your web-authoring software website.

You can also join the latest (as of mid-2004) Internet craze and start your own weblog. Blogging is not just the domain of late-night confessionalists and self-styled pundits. It has practical applications, too. In fact, one well-regarded website for a new resealable plastic storage bag used blogging to build "buzz" for the product (see Figure 9.5).

Blogs are a series of date-stamped entries on a webpage. Online blogging sites such as Movable Type, Blogger, and LiveJournal provide free and paid services that let you enter, categorize, archive and upload blog entries to your webserver with an easy-to-use web interface.

The world of computers is a world of acronyms and arcane technologies, and, of course, the web is a big part of it. Every one of them is good for something, but not everyone has a role in your small website. Here are few technologies you'll want to be familiar with as you embark on creating your successful small site:

- File Transfer Protocol (FTP, or SFTP, if secure transfer is provided by your Web host). This is the most common, but not the only, way to transfer web page files from your computer to your Web server. Typical FTP software (called a client) such as WS_FTP for Windows and Fetch for Macintosh present a point-and-click interface that allows you to upload files from your computer's hard drive to your webserver over your Internet connection. Web authoring software like Dreamweaver and GoLive have built-in FTP functionality and can even help you synchronize files between your hard drive and your webserver.

- The server-side include (SSI) is my favorite small-site technology. Includes are small text or HTML files that

Figure 9.5
The News section for the the Clip-n-Seal website is updated and published using blogging software.

Software such as NewzCrawler, NetNewsWire, and iBlog also provide a fill-in-the-blank desktop interface to the online services or can be configured to publish directly to your webserver. Blogging programs also double as blog readers (also called RSS readers, or newsfeed readers). Many large and not-so-large sites—such as the BBC, CNN, and NASA—publish updates as a feed, which can be compiled and viewed in a reader or syndicated for publication by another website.

As blogging and RSS feeds become more common, you may find a feed that complements your site and provides useful information to your visitors. Feedster.com and 2RSS.com are good places to keep tabs on the growing feed universe. But keep in mind that offering fresh content on your site through someone else's feed means putting someone else in charge of part of your site's content.

Automation options climb a steep nerd curve from here. Perl scripts, cookies, cron jobs, and automation logic written in a web-friendly scripting language within your webpages (see sidebar) are all common strategies used by sites to ease the burden of making frequent site updates by hand.

Anticipate Updates in Your Site Design

Up until now, the focus for this chapter has been on why updates are important, how often they should be done, and useful techniques for how to keep your site updated. Before we leave the topic of updates, we need to discuss some things that you should consider when designing your site in the first place so that your site will be easier to update.

First, let's review what on your site may need to be updated. I'm not talking about infrequent changes like your hours or phone number, but rather, the typical kinds of information that often goes out of date or needs to be supplemented, such as:

- News releases
- Sales and promotions
- Sponsored events
- Job openings or internships
- Meetings, trainings, or classes
- New clients and work samples
- Testimonials from satisfied customers
- Frequently asked questions
- Awards or recognitions
- Recalls or customer alerts
- Downloads
- Newsletters

The types of information you will need to update and the frequency with which you'll have to do it will have a strong bearing on certain aspects of your website's design. As I mentioned in Chapter 8, make sure you think through and account for all the updating you'll need to do on your site before your first meeting with your web designer. Or work with your web designer to identify the aspects of your business that will generate a need for site updates *before* you get too far along in the visual design process. You can almost literally paint yourself in a corner if you don't anticipate how updates will affect your site.

Decisions about color schemes and page formats can make or break the ease with which a site can handle updates. Text-heavy updates will work better on a site that uses dark text on a light background than vice-versa. Tight site designs (see Figure 9.6) may not be flexible enough to accommodate the updates you have in mind.

can be placed on a webpage with one line of code (called an include statement), allowing you to use and reuse the contents of the file on more than one page on your site. They are a great way to standardize your navigation bar, your page footer, or other elements of your site that you want to repeat on every page. When you need to make a change, you only have to update the include file.

Include files can contain any other HTML code (except other include tags) or be plain text. The technology is built into your webserver, but you may need to ask your Web host to add SSI parsing to your web pages. Often the default setting is to include files on webpages ending with .SHTML, but not .HTML. I recommend changing this so you can use includes on files ending with .HTML, too.

- Secure Sockets Layer (SSL) is the technology that allows a Web browser to make an encrypted connection to a webserver. Because information sent over the Internet usually makes several hops to get from point A to point B (allowing interlopers along the way to intercept the transmission), SSL ensures the contents can't be read when it contains confidential information such as a credit card number, Social Security number or password. You'll know you're using an SSL connection when the website address starts with "https" or you see a small, highlighted padlock icon in the corner of your browser window.

- CSS (cascading style sheets) is my second-favorite small-site technology, after server-side includes and tied with JavaScript, described below. Style sheets describe size, color, placement, and other attributes for elements on your webpages. For example, you might use a style sheet to indicate that all paragraphs (text enclosed by <p> and </p> tags) should be 10-point Arial. Like includes, style sheets are saved as one or more files on your server that can be referred to with one line of code in every page on your website. By centralizing design rules in one place, style sheets provide the dual benefit of reducing the size of your webpages (since you don't have to add "10-point Arial" to every <p> tag) and making redesigns and small design tweaks much easier.

- JavaScript is not Java. Tied with cascading style sheets as my second-favorite small site technology, JavaScript allows you to create dynamic HTML effects like image rollovers, errors messages

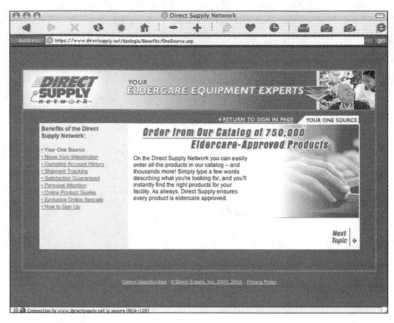

Figure 9.6
A site design that encloses the page contents with a border looks best when filled with small text chunks.

A good way to measure the impact of an update is to determine if a particular type of update will require a new page on your site. And if it requires a new page, it may also require some kind of navigation change. Adding a newsletter, news release, or job posting to your site will certainly require a new page. And if you want to make previous versions available through some kind of archive (generally, a good idea), then you'll need to leave room in your site design for some kind of secondary navigation that lets visitors click through to each of the old pages. Links like this can sometimes be indented under the primary navigation, displayed in a javascript drop-down menu, or listed as links in a special area of the page reserved for that use. If your designer wants to use graphics instead of text for page elements such as navigation buttons and headlines, make sure you get the original graphics files from him in case you need to make changes in a pinch.

Updates that don't require a new page or navigation are easier to accommodate in whatever site design you choose, but they'll have more impact on your visitors if you plan ahead (see Figure 9.7). Examples include a new menu download, a meeting or sale announcement or customer testimonial. As I mentioned earlier in this chapter, leave room in your home page design for short blurbs that visitors to your site can quickly scan for new information.

when forms are filled in incorrectly, and jump menus that let visitors quickly go to the page they're looking for, among many other cool, but functional, webpage enhancements. Most full-featured Web authoring software (Dreamweaver, GoLive) come with preprogrammed libraries of JavaScript code that you can add to your web pages.

Figure 9.7
The link to updated information (lower left) looks out-of-place on this otherwise good-looking site.

Summary

In this chapter you learned about the benefits of updating your site. Even a modest update schedule will help your site build an audience of repeat visitors and help you turn those visitors into customers. We also looked at some of the do's and don'ts of updating your site. Updating your site does not require redesigning your site. And in keeping with the small site philosophy, we found that more frequent updates do not necessary translate into more website success. You may discover as you update your site according to the guidelines of this chapter that your site has outgrown small site realm. We'll discuss what to do when you've outgrown your small site in Chapter 10.

What to Do When You've Outgrown a Small Site

10

- Learn the difference between overexpansion and measured growth.

- Learn to recognize the limitations of a small site.

- Learn techniques for reversing the course of a bloated site.

Websites grow and change—it's in their nature. A growing website is a good thing when its growth is managed correctly. Bloated sites, on the other hand, are obviously the result of website growth gone awry. Lacking a plan or a modicum of restraint or a sense of the resources involved in running a large website, small site owners too often allow unfocused content, unmanageable features, and irrelevant graphics to bog down their business's online presence.

In this chapter, we'll discuss the reasons you might need to expand your site beyond the Small Site model, as well as when to do it and how to do it right. We'll review what a small site is and what it's not, compared with a bloated site. You'll learn about the limitations of a small site and the difference between overexpansion and deliberate, well-planned growth. You'll also learn how to keep your site from becoming bloated and how to anticipate and manage site growth. And if your site is already bloated, we'll look at what you can do to reverse course.

Reasons You May Outgrow a Small Site

After you build a small site that follows the model presented in this book, the day may come when you'll want to expand it—either because of changes in your business or in spite of them.

You may have held back with the first version of your site, waiting for it (and the effort you put into it) to prove its worth to your business. When that happens, you might want to show off more of your business on your site.

Or your business may have grown, helped in part by your website. You may find that the increased traffic to your site justifies new website tools, features, or services that didn't make sense when your business and your site were small.

Or it may simply be that the expansion of your business leaves you less time than ever to devote to your site at a time when it could benefit most from your attention. The challenge you'll face in these situations is in knowing where and when to stay true to the Small Site philosophy and how and why to take your small site to the next level.

Small Sites and Bloated Sites—What They Are and What They Are Not

When I introduced the Small Site concept in Chapter 1, I made clear distinctions between big sites and bloated sites and between small sites and boring sites. Big does not mean bloated and small does not mean boring.

Small sites need not be small in scope, though many businesses can maximize their web success with a site as small as one page. The Small Site philosophy instead revolves around building focused sites that meet customers' needs online where possible, offer offline alternatives where they can't, and provide their owners with a structured, resource-respecting, easy-to-update Web presence that doesn't break the bank.

Bloated sites usually have many more pages than they need, but the high page count isn't the only contributor to the bloat. In other words, bloated sites share common traits regardless of their size. They are out of control and lack meaningful ways to track or measure their effectiveness. Like an SUV full of super-sized passengers, they suck up more than their fair share of resources—money spent on web designers and hosting services, plus the head-scratching time their keepers spend trying to figure out how to maintain and update them. Lacking focus, design discipline, and customer-oriented content and functionality, bloated sites make enemies with the people that try to use them and the owners that try to maintain them.

A small site is always a better choice for a small, local business, especially one that's just getting started. But small sites have their limits, too. In general, small sites fall short in their ability to scale. That means what works on a site of five pages and a few hundred page views a month probably won't work for a site of 50 (or more) pages and thousands of page views a month.

Here are some small site attributes that you'll likely have to abandon when your site grows:

- Small sites are best managed by one person—or at most two people who preferably share an office (or even a computer) and can stay in close contact about the maintenance of the site. Large sites—by definition—require more time for posting updates and correcting errors as they come up. Small sites are best updated at a moderate rate, such as once a week or less frequently. If your site grows with your business, you'll need to enlist some help and begin thinking about a site management or content management system (which we'll come back to later in this chapter).

- Small sites provide a business with an economical way to communicate *asynchronously* with its customers and potential customers. That means you and your visitors need not be online at the same time for your site's message to get to them and for them to contact you through forms or email links on the site.

- Small sites aren't designed to facilitate customers sharing information with each other or solving each other's problems while online through advanced site features such as online bulletin boards and live web chat. If your business has grown to the point where such website features make sense, you're going to need a bigger site.

- Small sites are good for selling a limited product selection through non–shopping cart order forms or outsourced e-commerce tools. Offering a large online catalog through a small site can generate all manner of headaches, from keeping up with fulfillment to tracking down availability and pricing disparities with offline inventory.

- Small sites can extend the marketing efforts of a small business rather than being a business onto themselves. For example, a business that peddles T-shirts with nostalgic pop culture sayings for aging Gen Xers might start out posting flyers in coffee shops around town, hawking its wares at weekend arts festivals, and maintaining a small website that lists a handful of local shops that sell the shirts. But if the GenXTs.com website takes off, the small site the business started with likely won't meet the needs of visitors or the booming business behind it.

Anticipate and Manage Site Growth without Getting Bloated

Any business owner would be glad to have the problem of a business that outgrows its website. But too often, the limitations of small sites are addressed by their owners in ways that lead to bloat (see Figure 10.1). A familiar scenario goes like this: Someone builds a small site that captures a particular stage in the life of a business—a start-up, new management, a new logo, or a new name. The owner is happy, the web designer gets paid, and a modest number of visitors find the site and use it to contact the business or learn more about it.

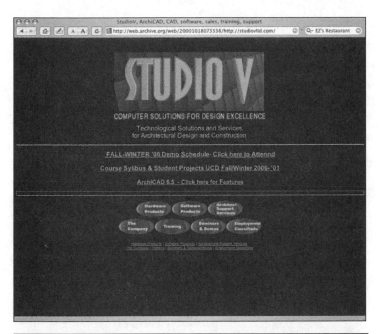

Figure 10.1
A software company website circa 2001 (top)—a well-behaved
small site. A recent visit reveals that the site has not aged well.

But then the business succeeds, and with success comes changes. The business may add locations, employees, new products, or all of the above and more. It may enter new markets or diversify as it grows. Additions like these require new website pages, or maybe a new website altogether.

If you've come to realize that your small site no longer represents your business, you have a handful of options to consider—from doing nothing to embarking on a complete site overhaul. Each brings with it a potential for bloat, from minimal to extreme. As you consider your choices, keep in mind these general pitfalls to avoid in order to keep your site from getting bloated:

- **Don't try to do too much**. Move slowly and stick with your focus. A small site needs a theme or objective that helps first-time visitors quickly understand the site's purpose. Doubling your business's sales or adding a new location doesn't necessarily require a website that's twice as big, especially if the extra pages dilute or cloud your site's focus. Don't use your site to "try something out." Your site is not a "trial balloon."

- **Don't try to design (or redesign) your site as you go**. If accommodating your business's growth on your website requires deviating from your site's design or bending the rules too far on what goes where, then you need to rethink your strategy for managing your website's growth.

- **Don't ignore your site**. Browse the pages and test your feedback forms regularly. Add updates regularly—even if it's something small. Tie up loose ends on your website promptly. Don't leave old offers or news on the site; they'll confuse your visitors and waste your time as you try to undo the confusion.

Option No. 1: Do Nothing
Bloat Risk: Low

We've all come across sites on the Web that for one reason or another have become frozen in time (see Figure 10.2). As a long-time web designer, I find these abandoned sites to be curious artifacts of the Internet's past, and they are fascinating to me the way the ruins of lost civilizations prove fascinating for archaeologists. Unfortunately, letting virtual dust collect on a site doesn't help the business. Websites that don't change with the business they represent might as well not exist.

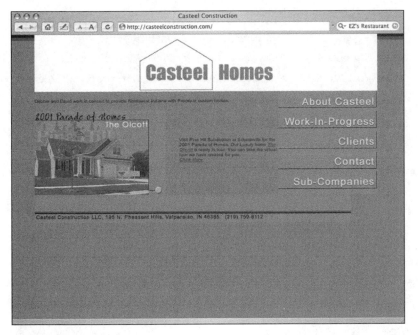

Figure 10.2
The Casteel Homes website trumpets the construction company's participation in the 2001 Parade of Homes. Too bad this screen shot was made in the summer of *2004*.

Obviously, you minimize the chance that your site will become bloated if you leave it small while your business grows. But the downside is that your site will slowly become less relevant to visitors and less representative of your business. You'll have to do something eventually. And when you finally do, it might be too late.

Option No. 2: Add Content to Existing Pages

Bloat Risk: Low to Moderate

Even a small site should have some room for expansion. If your site expansion can be accomplished by adding content to the pages you already have, then you stand a good chance of avoiding bloat, especially if you have closely followed the Small Site model and have the self-control to stick to the plan.

If you have identified a focus for your site, you know the kinds of new content that will augment your small site's purpose and what will blur it. If you have taken the time to format your pages for scannability with bullet lists, subheads, and short paragraphs, you should apply the same methods to abridge new content for the unique needs of web readers.

Changing or expanding your site to reflect your business's growth while keeping it small requires the same discipline you exercised when you designed the site. But you're not limited to adding to existing pages. Variations on this theme include reorganizing content on existing pages, moving content from one existing page to another, or removing unnecessary pages and replacing them with new, more relevant pages or content.

You can even rename navigation items to more accurately reflect the pages they lead to. For example, if your business has grown from one location to two, change your "Contact Us" link to "Locations"; if you've expanded your online order form from one product to three or four, change the "Order" link to say "Products."

Option No. 3: Split Your Growing Site into Two New Small Sites

Bloat Risk: Moderate

You might find yourself in a situation in which two small sites are better than one big site. Each site can remain true to the Small Site model, and a landing page (here's really good place to use one) can direct visitors to the site that represents the division of your business they're looking for (see Figure 10.3).

For example, say you once only sold the widgets and now you're advising other companies on which widgets to buy and training their employees in how to use the widgets they already own. A small site likely can't serve both sides of your business equally well. The solution: Divide your growing site into two new small sites. For example, acmewidgets.com might subdivide into acmewidgetsales.com and acmewidgetconsulting.com. Figure 10.4 presents another example of how this technique can be used to subdivide a site.

Option No. 4: Add New Pages or Features to Current Site

Bloat Risk: Moderate to High

You might try to expand your site incrementally or with a piecemeal approach—the "design-as-you-go" method. That's often the unavoidable choice a harried business owner faces if they want a site that keeps up with their business. It's also a strategy that exposes a site to an acute bloat infection, and the results usually aren't pretty.

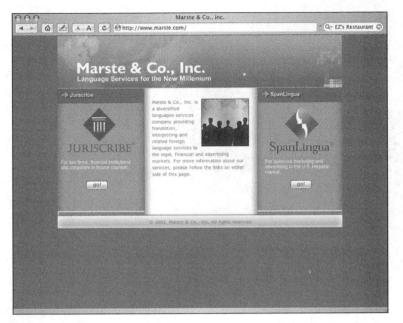

Figure 10.3
Marste & Co. provides language services to the legal and Hispanic marketing industries and offers a home page that guides visitors to the subsite that meets their needs.

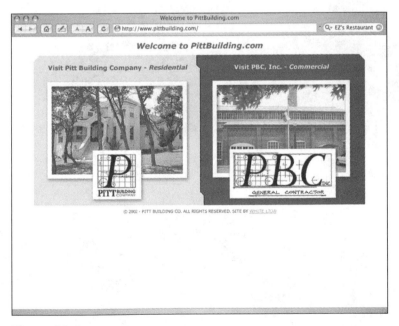

Figure 10.4
A construction company offers separate sites for its residential and commercial businesses.

Website builders often let the latest thing take over as most important, even if it doesn't fit into the overall theme or focus of a site. The site ends up having all the appeal of an eight-headed monster (see Figure 10.5).

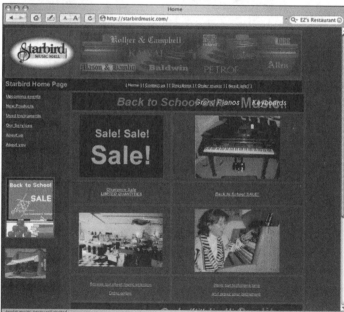

Figure 10.5
The Starbird Music home page, circa 2000 (top) is a simple affair, if a little bit too text heavy. The current version (bottom) appears to suffer from feature-itis.

The best defense against runaway design is to keep your small site's focus in mind and use a design template to maintain consistency. Your small site may not meet your business's needs forever. But by staying true to the theme and format you established when you created it, you'll be better prepared to know when the time is right to undertake a more substantial redesign when that time comes.

Option No. 5: Start Over with a New Site
Bloat Risk: Low to Moderate

When properly cared for and maintained, a small site can be a beneficial adjunct to a small business for many years. But sometimes the only good way to expand a site is to start over. Even small, successful websites have a shelf life, typically somewhere between 18 months and 4 years. When the time comes to redesign (and if you're committed to using the Web to strengthen your business, it will), you'll have the advantage of applying what you learned both from this book and from the first site you built to create a new site that reflects how your business has changed.

You can create new pages, rearrange navigation, add to or modify your site's focus, and build in new tools and other features from the beginning without encountering the specter of bloat. Figure 10.6 shows a good example of a site that got itself into a bloated state and then was redesigned. Notice how clean the redesign looks.

Turn Your Bloated Site into a Successful Small Site

No one sets out to create a bloated site. They just seem to happen. For small business owners, the Web's indeterminate boundaries and their own limited time for managing a site often combine to make bloat hard to avoid. Such clutter-inducing circumstances probably describe the desks, offices, and vehicles of a few of you!

SHOULD I SWITCH TO A DYNAMIC SITE, A STATIC SITE, OR A HYBRID?

Dynamic websites driven by content management systems are easy to identify. If the webpage address ends with a suffix like .cgi, .php, or .asp followed by a question mark and other parameters that help the system build the page, you're looking at a dynamic site that uses some kind of content management system.

Web pages on dynamic sites are designed on-the-fly by the web server using content stored in a database. The opposite of a dynamic site is a static site. Static sites are not sites that never change; pages on static sites—and that's most sites on the Web—can't be changed unless someone saves an updated copy of the HTML file on the server.

Dynamic sites have their own unique pluses and minuses. A dynamic site can grow much more easily and be managed much more efficiently by a group of people than a small static site can.

On the other hand, dynamic sites often end up with a cookie-cutter look—they can enforce consistency to a fault. Content management systems also can be expensive and changes may require the expertise of a programmer.

As the need to grow or even redesign your site increases, you might think about building it using a content management system. But it doesn't need to be an all-or-nothing decision. Consider a hybrid approach—part static, part dynamic. Dynamic pages are a great platform for site content that changes frequently: product pages, FAQs, news releases, and the like. If you can count on one hand the number of times a page on your site changes in a year, leave it static. With a few code tweaks (which should be within the capabilities of an experienced web designer), your site's page template can guide the format of both your dynamic and static pages.

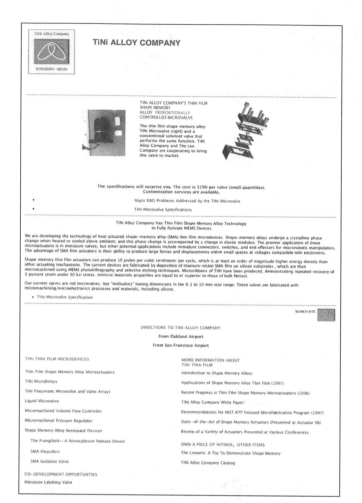

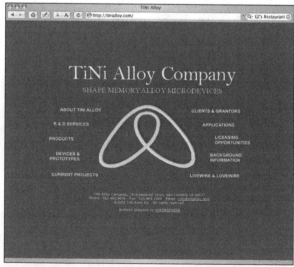

Figure 10.6
The TiNi Alloy website of a few years back (top) and its redesigned counterpart (bottom).

But while disorder can be excused in your personal spaces, it can't be forgiven on your website. Your website puts an inexpensive and effective public face on your business. Just because you know where everything is on your site and how it works doesn't mean anyone else does, or that they care to spend the time to figure it out.

Un-bloating a site requires a "keep or toss" mentality. Keep website pages and features that adhere to your small site focus and provide visitors with the essential information they are seeking. Toss out anything that slows down your site, confuses visitors, and can't be (or hasn't been) maintained and updated easily and efficiently. Start by taking an inventory of everything on your site.

Take Stock of What You Have

Create a table using a spreadsheet program or just use old-fashioned pen and paper and make a list of all the pages on your site. When you're done, you'll have an overview of your site that can form the basis of a plan to remove pages and/or reorganize the ones you keep. In the first column, identify each page by its name—either the page title or headline, whichever makes the most sense—and by its place on your site (directory and filename). Boldface or otherwise highlight the main navigation pages, and list their subpages underneath them. Across the top, make columns for the following questions.

- **When was the page created and for whom?** When was it last updated? If you can't remember (or think of a good reason) why a page is on your site, then that page is probably contributing to your site's bloat.

- **Does the page load fast enough, or is it too slow?** Give slow pages a second or third try on consecutive days to eliminate the possibility that network sluggishness is the culprit rather than page bloat.

- **Who's responsible for updating the page, how often, and how long does it take?** For interactive site features like feedback forms, you should also make a note of how much support time (for reading responses, testing the form) the feature requires.

- **What other pages on the site does the page link to?** Do those links do something other than open another web page, such as download a file or create a new email message? What offsite links are listed on the page?

- **Does the page have any special features, such as opening in a pop-up window or requiring a plug-in to display properly?** These features not only contribute to bloat but they can be really annoying to visitors who come to your site.

- **Do you make use of your site statistics?** If your web host keeps traffic statistics about your site and you (or your web designer) can get access to the processed page view tallies from the server logs, add that information to the mix. Consider a significant but manageable time frame, say, the two or three most recent complete months. If you have pages on your site that you know (or suspect) have seasonal traffic spikes, include that information, too.

With your site's vitals in hand, a picture will emerge that can guide you in sweeping away clutter. Are the pages that require the most effort being seen by enough visitors to your site to justify the time you spend on them? Are the most popular pages being updated often enough? If most of the visitors to your site are finding old information, you might need to shift your site resources to those pages.

- **Have you optimized your images?** On slow-loading pages, optimize and remove unnecessary images and replace text set as images with plain HTML.

- **Is your site traffic uneven?** If site traffic is spread out or concentrated on the wrong pages, consolidate your navigation to 8 to 10 categories or fewer. Move less-popular sections under your main sections or remove them altogether if they are outside the site's focus or simply outdated. Make sure visitors can get to the most popular pages on your site from all the other most popular pages.

- **Is your site traffic lacking?** If you have healthy site traffic but you're not getting the response from your site you hoped for, do a little homegrown user testing. Ask a friend who never or only rarely uses your website to find five critical pieces of information about your business—are they the five you want visitors to remember? Or ask a friend or two to spend a minute on your site and then tell you what they remember about your site. Is your site guiding visitors to the call to action you want them to find? If you're feeling bold, take your show on the road. Quiz strangers at an Internet café. Offer them coupons or specials at your business in exchange for feedback.

- **Do you think you need to start over?** You might find that the easiest way to heal a bloated site is by starting over, but that may not be an option if you don't have the time and money to make it happen. Instead, spend the time to figure out where the problems are and address them.

In the end, your site is only as good as the time and thought you put into it. Don't be afraid to drop, delete, or just rearrange pages that don't benefit your business or improve your website. Chances are they won't be missed.

Summary

In this chapter, you learned how to gauge when a small site may no longer meet the needs of your growing and changing business. We reviewed the strengths and weaknesses of small sites in order to understand strategies for expanding your site. Presented with a range of real-world options, you saw the different ways that you can avoid—or invite—bloat when small sites expand. Finally, you learned methods for eradicating bloat and getting their sites back on the Small Site path.

SMALL SITES FOR
PROFESSIONAL SERVICES

11

- Learn how to create a small
  site for a professional business such as a doctor,
  dentist or architect.

In Chapters 1 through 10 we covered all of the key design techniques and strategies for creating small sites. For the remainder of this book we'll now turn our attention to exploring a set of small sites that have been designed for different professions. My hope is that these different sites will provide you with ideas and inspiration that you can use to create our modify your own site. Our first close-up look at model small sites will focus on sites for professional services.

The purveyors of professional services may go by one of a number of common names—lawyer, doctor, dentist, architect—but their area of specialization differentiates their services and helps them build a successful practice. For example, a children's dentist may have more in common with a health care provider for other types of services for children than someone who specializes in general dentistry.

If your business provides a professional service, it's important to design your small site around the unique needs of your potential customers. And the more specialized your service is, the more your site needs a specialized focus. A potential client who finds your website is likely looking for an expert in a particular field. Perhaps they have a new baby on the way and need an attorney for estate planning or an architect who specializes in residential remodeling to add in a much needed extra bedroom. In other words, they already have a job in mind for you when they find your site. It's your job to design your site so that you anticipate the needs of your customers given the specialization that you provide.

SITE WALK-THROUGH: DRVERABROWN.COM

Let's take a closer look at how a professional site can be designed to anticipate the needs of the potential clients who access it. Here we'll do a walk-through of a successful site for an Oregon dentist (see Figure 11.1).

What I Like: The color scheme is subdued and inviting and the doctor's picture presents her as friendly and competent. The before and after images on the right of the home page (top screen), while not necessarily appealing, are definitely eye-catching and offer a nice visual testimonial of the doctor's work. Critical information about the practice, such as the doctor's degree and phone number, are easy to spot, and the "Smile Gallery" is a novel, yet still obvious, way to label the doctor's page of work samples.

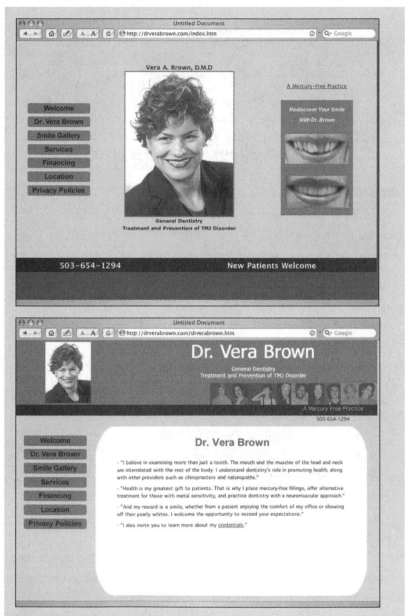

Figure 11.1
An Oregon dentist's website does a nice job of introducing its practice.

What I Would Change: The link referring to the doctor's avoidance of mercury fillings distinguishes her practice for a significant subset of health-conscious potential patients. I would make the link more prominent, perhaps by having a designer create a small logo to call attention to this distinctive aspect of the practice. The home page needs keyword and description tags to help search engine placement, and "mercury-free practice" is a phrase that should be included in them. I would suggest two refinements for the left-hand navigation buttons: On the home page, remove "Welcome" since it links to the home page itself. The second button—"Dr. Vera Brown"—could be clearer if labeled "Philosophy" because that better reflects the contents of that subpage. I would also use the same large version of the doctor's name as a header on the home page and on the subpages.

Answering the Call

Your website can help people screen themselves by screening you. Visitors to a professional services website need to quickly determine if the services offered are a match for their needs. A site that focuses on how your area of specialization meets their needs can be the first step in a satisfying relationship for both you and your client.

Visitors to your site probably won't add it to their bookmarks. In fact, they may never go to your site again. But a successful visit to your website can't be measured in site traffic alone. A visit to your site should ideally lead to a phone call or in-person consultation at your office.

This is the one reason that a professional site doesn't need a lot of extra information or clutter. The focus should be on emphasizing the unique service that you provide, how you can be contacted, your office hours, and your credentials—the really important bits of information that help a visitor match their unique needs with your service.

Home-Page Helper

Your site visitors are looking to form a long-term relationship, to spend a bundle on a one-time dose of your expertise, or both. The contents of your home page should help visitors quickly determine if you practice the specialty that they're seeking. On top of that, your home page should emphasize your trustworthiness and expertise.

What type of law or medicine do you practice? What projects or assignments are your specialty? Call attention to your areas of expertise with a bullet list, or boldface a few key words in a short description of your practice (see Figure 11.2).

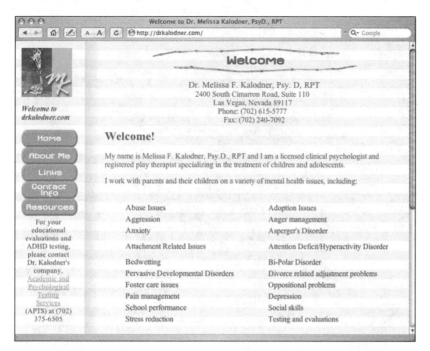

Figure 11.2
The conditions that Dr. Kalodner, a Las Vegas psychologist, treats are clearly listed on her home page, along with her address and other contact information.

Back up your claims with the *imprimatur* of a higher authority: the bar exams you've passed, the board certifications you hold, the state agencies with which you're registered, the governing bodies with which you're affiliated, and degree you hold and the school you got it from.

SITE WALK-THROUGH: SBRA.COM

Let's take inside look at another small site designed to promote a professional service. This time we'll perform our walk-through of an architect's site (see Figure 11.3).

What I Like: The home page presents several well-packaged elements that support the business's qualifications and expertise: a recent award gets prominence on the left side of the page, a quote from an well-known trade group attests to the firm's skills, and an array of images illustrate a variety of project specialties. Aligning the primary navigation links, which switch from white to yellow when moused over, along the curve adds a bit of flair for a profession that trades on style and impression.

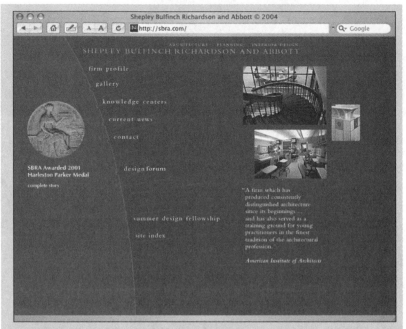

Figure 11.3
A Boston architectural firm's site nicely balances function and elegance.

What I Would Change: Not much. The work sample images on the home page could be linked to larger versions or a page of other views of the same project. The gaps in the main navigation reflect organizational distinctions that may be clearer to the site builder than the site visitors. To avoid any confusion about the gaps being missing or unloaded images, the primary navigation might be better arranged as a continuous list of links.

Finally, give people a reason to trust you. Are you someone with whom your clients will feel comfortable sharing their most private secrets? Put your picture on your home page to help them decide.

Killer App

Many professionals use a variety of pen-and-paper questionnaires or surveys to assess the needs of potential clients. On your website, a screening form can accomplish some of the same goals while also informing visitors about how their problem can (or can't) be addressed by your specialty.

However, don't expect your visitors to muddle through the same 42-question form online that you give them offline. Create an abbreviated version—5 to 7 questions plus contact information—that's just enough to let you measure online interest in your business and track potential clients. On the page that thanks them for completing the form, offer the opportunity to download the long version so they can complete it before your first face-to-face meeting.

The Word Is Out

It's important to put as much attention as you can into novel ways to get people to your site.

Because their titles are common and (relatively) easy-to-spell words, professional service providers can attract potential clients to their site by taking advantage of a common Web browsing behavior: surfers who cast about on the Web by typing in web addresses that might have a chance of bringing up a live website. Call it "URL fishing meets URL hoarding."

For example, a psychologist on the north side of Chicago might spend a hundred dollars or so to register""lincolnparktherapist.com" and a dozen other variations that combine locales and familiar occupational monikers in domain names that get forwarded to her actual website. A lawyer in Bloomington, Indiana, might want to exploit regional school loyalty with "hoosierlawyer.com." (See Figure 11.4 for some more examples.)

Keep It Small

Avoid the tendency to weigh down your home page with too much information. You offer a sophisticated service, and an overwhelming home page can intimidate some of your potential clients.

Figure 11.4
Easy-to-remember domain names can add extra
oomph to your online marketing: A fertility clinic
delivers its site at haveababy.com (top). Prospective
patients of a West Coast therapist can make a
mental note of her site (middle): lashrink.com. And
a Boston-area dental practice fills online queries at
dentalemergency.net (bottom).

SITE WALK-THROUGH: SAHILTON.COM

For our next walk-through, we'll explore a small site that features a Realtor (see Figure 11.5).

What I Like: Many of the important ingredients are present: A studio portrait, contact information at the top of the page, a short bio, a list of professional affiliations, and the logo of a well-known national real estate firm. All of these combine to establish credibility and attract prospective clients. The main links on the site—"Buyers and Sellers," "Relocating," and "Search MLS"—lead to succinct subpages. I assumed the first time I looked at this site that the "Search MLS" link would lead me off to some other site—a navigation no-no—but it doesn't. Instead, the subpage explains what MLS (Multiple Listing Service) is, then gives visitors the option of proceeding offsite to search for properties that meet their criteria.

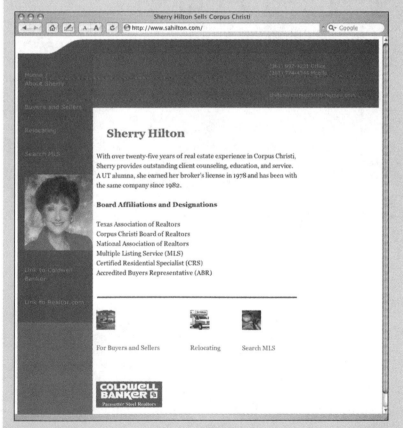

Figure 11.5
A Texas Realtor's site covers the essentials but still leaves room for improvement.

What I Would Change: I think the gray on blue and gray on gray color scheme makes the navigation hard to read. I would switch to white or even yellow on gray or blue to make those components of the design pop out from the background. I also think the Realtor's portrait and name (and perhaps the firm's logo) should be combined in a new, more prominent page header, which would strengthen the site's brand.

SITE WALK-THROUGH: LEBARI.COM

For our final professional site walk-through, we'll examine a lawyer's site that is well-designed (see Figure 11.6).

What I Like: Better-than-average clip art photos—the gavel and courthouse steps—reinforce the nature of the site, while the faded and enlarged logo in the main content section adds a touch of branding—"lawyer" starts with "L" after all. Each of the firm's specialties is clearly listed and linked in the main section of the home page. The subpages present succinctly formatted text that's easy to scan, and each page lists the firm's full contact information at the bottom.

What I Would Change: The lower-left third of the home page offers search boxes for finding law-related sites on the Web. I suspect those get more use by the firm's staff than by potential clients visiting the site. I would relegate them to a subpage. The specialty links would be easier to scan if they were presented as a bullet list as the subpages are.

The Professional Services Small Site Design Checklist

Here's a handy checklist to use to help you design your own professional services small site.

- Your primary goal is to get potential customers to call or contact you, so make sure that your contact information is very accessible. If at all possible, put your contact information on your home page or at least provide a link to the contact information from the home page.

- Clearly list the range of services you provide, but make sure you state your area of specialization very concisely and accurately. Don't fall into the trap of trying to be too general.

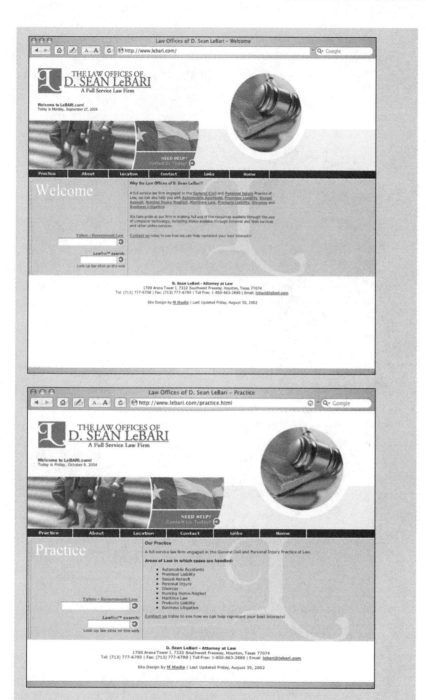

Figure 11.6
This attorney's site, while a bit bigger and more polished than your typical small site, offers evidence in how to make a case for your business online.

- To keep from cluttering up your important message, avoid trying to display too much information on your site (see Figure 11.7). Providing a link to a newsletter or a newsletter itself in PDF format that the user can download is fine, but just make sure that support information like this doesn't get in the way of your real message.

Figure 11.7
Visitors to a commercial Realtor's site might be overwhelmed by the volume of information presented on the home page.

- Clearly display the credentials that you have.

- Provide testimonials to enhance your credentials.

- If you work with a network of other professionals who provide services related to yours, provide information about this. You might want to include a "related professional services" page. This will help show a potential customer that you are part of an established community of service professionals.

- If you have received awards or favorable press, provide the information or links to the sites or publications that are appropriate.

- Try to keep your home page really simple. Remember that potential customers who come to your site are likely searching for a professional service and that they've probably seen other sites before they get to yours.

- Spend some time looking at other sites providing professional services that compete with yours.

- Avoid complicated navigation features. This is not where you want to show off the latest website design techniques.

- If you employ the services of a web designer to create a service-oriented site for you, make sure that the designer has experience in creating the type of site that you need. Don't let the designer get carried away in adding features you really don't need.

Summary

In this chapter we took a close-up look at useful techniques for creating small sites for professional services. The most critical thing we learned is that just as professionals specialize in certain areas, their sites need to as well. A good professional site must attract clients who are looking for services that meet their unique needs—and not a "one size fits all" site.

SMALL SITES FOR TRADE SERVICES 12

- Learn how to create a specialized site for a trade service.

Unlike with yellow pages listings, where ad size and alphabetical ordering can extend an advantage to one business over another, competition among websites starts on a more level playing field. Within the confines of a typical browser window—800x600 pixels, more or less—a web surfer is just as likely to find a trade services site located across town as they are to find one across the street.

Even as more of your potential customers let their browsers do the walking, the questions they want answered when selecting someone for the job remain the same: Are you competent? Do you repair the brand I own? Do you work in my area? How much do you charge? How soon can you do the work? Your site has to convince a potential customer that you're the right one for the job.

Your site also has to address the concerns of visitors who may know a friend or neighbor who has been burned by someone in your line of work. They may have suffered themselves, so it's safe to say that caution and doubt are common attitudes among many of the visitors to your site.

Answering the Call

A visit to your website should lead to a service call, an in-home visit, or a trip to your shop. You might even get a few visitors who bookmark your site for future reference or to refer a friend.

You'll have even better results attracting repeat visitors if you spend the time to develop a plan for updating your site on a regular basis as I explained in Chapter 9. Updating a trade service website need not be a weekly, or even monthly, chore. A quarterly update, based on seasonal changes, can be enough. For example, as cold weather approaches, a landscaper could offer a few tips for winterizing lawns and gardens. A plumber could explain how to prevent pipes from freezing.

But before you think about how your site can meet the needs of returning visitors, you must make sure it gives first-timers the answers to basic questions about the way you do business because they will probably make up the majority of your site traffic.

Home-Page Helper

People want to learn something about you and your business from your site. What's more, your small site home page should focus on conveying trustworthiness and competence and answering yes to the question, Can you do the job?

For businesses that make house calls, a picture of yourself in front of your repair truck can be an effective graphic for your home page (see Figure 12.1). The benefit? Customers will have confidence that your business is legitimate and they'll recognize you when you pull into the driveway. (The dog may bark anyway.)

You also should have a list of the products you install, service, and repair so people can easily determine that you've got the tools and know-how for the job. Brand logos—when sized and arranged discreetly in a corner or along one side of the page—can augment the effect (see Figure 12.2). But beware the bloat potential here: Too many logos placed indiscriminately on the page will result in a cluttered design.

Figure 12.1
Good choices for home page graphics on trade services sites: a photograph of a work sample or your service vehicle.

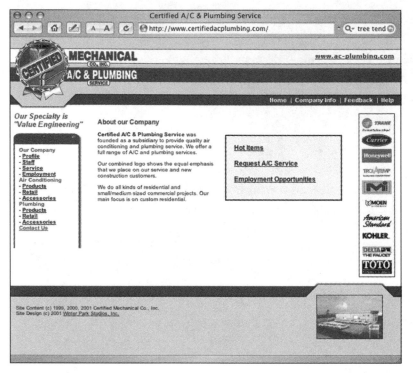

Figure 12.2
Manufacturers' logos come in all shapes, sizes, and colors. Spending the time and money to arrange the ones for the companies your business deals with in a neat row on your site (right side of screen) has two benefits: They look more professional when presented this way and they give potential customers a quick visual cue about the type of work your business can handle.

Finally, customers want to know if you can get to them or if they can get to you. Use MapQuest or Expedia to create a map and put it on a page with a list of zip codes you serve or major roads that delineate your service area. If you run a repair shop in a part of town unfamiliar to your customers, put a picture of your shop on your site so they can pick you out among your neighbors.

Make sure your site's meta tags—the hidden code that helps search engines categorize and summarize your site—include key phrases about your service area. You're better off trying to think of all the regional permutations that a potential customer might use to find you—neighborhood names and the like—than in making sure that your marketing slogan shows up in search results.

Killer App

If you run a repair business for a living, you probably live out of your van or repair truck and have gone through so many padded earpiece covers for your cell phone that you're thinking about buying them in bulk. And your spouse is probably giving you hard time about talking *and writing* while driving. Such is the life of a modern tradesman—taking calls for new business while shuttling from one job to the next.

What if your website could make your life easier and your customers' experience better? Here's how: Put a form on your site that emails a text message to your cell phone or beeper. Most cell phone accounts have an associated email address for receiving text messages, something like 5551212@yourphoneco.com.

If you're not the high-tech type, you might pay a web designer a couple hundred dollars to set it up for you. Three or four "fields"—or questions—should do the trick: a name, callback number, the nature of the problem, and the urgency.

Leave your hands free to drive and let your website field your customer calls for you.

The Word Is Out

You've got your website address painted on your truck and printed on your invoices and yellow pages ad. You may even have a magnetic sign affixed to your off-hours vehicle. But few people have a computer handy to type in web addresses as they see them in the yellow pages or on the side of a truck.

Of course, a tried-and-true way to build a business is through word of mouth. And the best time to get people to your site is when they're already online. So combine the two. Many towns, neighborhoods, and citizens groups have community email lists—hosted by Yahoo! Groups and the like—where recommendations spread like an undiscovered leak under the floorboards.

Instead of or in addition to collecting testimonials from satisfied customers, ask them to post positive messages about you on neighborhood email lists. Or be proactive (but not boastful) by posting timely tips or helpful reminders to the list now and then. And make sure you have your business name and website address in your email signature.

SITE WALK-THROUGH: PINNACLELOCK.COM

In this walk-through, we'll look at a Phoenix-area locksmith's site (see Figure 12.3).

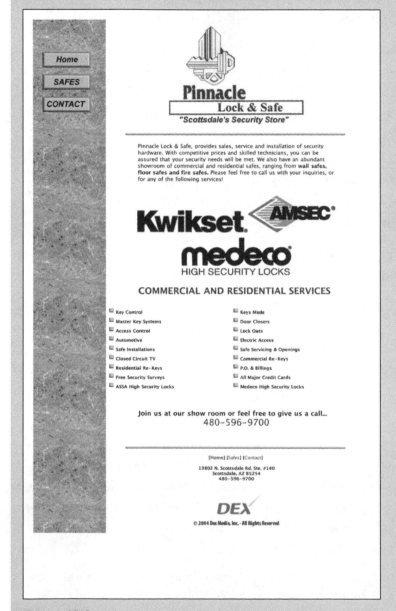

Figure 12.3
This Phoenix-area locksmith does a good job of providing its potential customers with a list of provided services.

What I Like: The site designer knows the limits of the site in a good way. Rather than offering visitors a contact form that the owners might not have to time to answer or an extensive online catalog that the owners might not be able to keep up-to-date, the site encourages visitors to pick up the phone and call to get more information. The major design elements present a good overview of the business without being overwhelming: three navigation choices, a logo that incorporates information about the service area (Scottsdale), visual cues that show brands sold, and a bullet list of services offered.

What I Would Change: The layout should be condensed so that more of the good information on the home page appears in the first screen. The screenshot shown here is about two screens' worth of information on a typical visitor's monitor. The logo could be rearranged in a more horizontal orientation by repositioning the words to the right of the key graphic rather than beneath it. The brand logos could be scaled down in size without reducing their impact, and doing so would make room for adding other brand logos. Visitors shouldn't have to scroll to see the phone number and call to action. The site also should list business hours so people will know when there will be someone available to take their call.

Keep It Small

Resist the urge to overstuff your site with unnecessary features that will do nothing to defuse any negative opinions your visitors may have about people in your line of work.

The Trade Services Small Site Checklist

Here's a handy checklist to use to help you design your own trade services small site.

- Your primary goal is to reassure potential customers who may feel there is nothing that differentiates your business—good or bad—from your competitors. Stating information such as how many years you've been in business, a Better Business Bureau seal of approval, and whether your business is bonded and insured can go a long way toward addressing those concerns.

- Clearly display the credentials that you have, especially state or local licensing information. Be sure to familiarize yourself with any regulations that might *require* this type of information to be on your site. Either way, it's a good idea to include it, along with a list of the brands you service or other industry certifications you've received.

- In general, people know what kind of work electricians and roofers do, so a full list of services you provide may not be necessary. If you offer any unique or specialized services that most of your competitors do not offer—for example, offering well-digging services if you're a plumber—make sure that information is highlighted on your home page.

- Give people some idea of how much your services cost, either with specific dollar amounts or general information about package pricing or your policies for charging by the hour or by the project. Consider offering a free consultation or discount to website visitors. (And remember that people who really want to know how much you charge will figure out a way to find out.)

- Provide testimonials from satisfied customers to enhance your credentials. Two easy-to-harvest sources for these are emails you receive from satisfied customers and well-worded recommendations posted on local email lists. (For more about testimonials, see Chapter 5.)

- If you work with a network of other trade businesses who provide services related to yours, provide information about this. You might want to include a "related services" page. This will help show a potential customer that you are part of an established community of service providers.

- Try to keep your home page really simple. Remember that potential customers who come to your site are likely searching for a service and that they've probably seen other sites before they get to yours.

- Spend some time looking at other sites providing trade services that are competitive with yours.

- Avoid complicated navigation features. This is not where you want to show off the latest website design techniques.

- If you employ the services of a web designer to create a service-oriented site for you, make sure the designer has experience in creating the type of site you need. Don't let the designer get carried away in adding features you really don't need.

SITE WALK-THROUGH: SSPOOLS.COM

In this walk-through, we'll look at a Nashville pool and construction company website (see Figure 12.4).

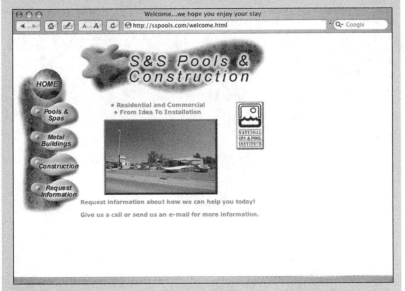

Figure 12.4
This pool construction company provides another useful model of a trade-specific website.

What I Like: The site offers proof that simplicity and fun can coexist. The water motif in the logo and navigation, while not likely to win any design awards (that I know of), does a good job of visually confirming the nature of the business without impeding the site's usability. The easy-to-read black navigation text leads to subpages with useful information for visitors considering the company's products and services. Likewise, the simple and easy-to-remember domain name (sspools.com) is a better online address for the site than syllable-rich alternatives such as s-s-pools.com or s-and-s-pools.com. (For more on choosing a domain name for your site, see Chapter 6.)

What I Would Change: Even a pool and spa company doesn't need a splash screen entry page, but this site has one (not shown). All it does is put an uninformative and extraneous step between the actual site and its visitors. On the real home page, I'd like to see a slide show of work samples rather than a photo of what appears to be the outside of the company's showroom. Location shots are helpful when paired with a physical address, hours of operation, and even a street map. On this site, a new navigation item and subpage called "Visit Us" would be ideal for this information.

SITE WALK-THROUGH: TOTALBRICKPAVERS.COM

In this walk-through, we'll look at a two-page site for an Orlando brick paving company (see Figure 12.5).

Figure 12.5
This company does a good job of displaying its specialized trade service.

What I Like: The site doesn't try to do too much, a smart move for a business whose employee(s) probably spend most of their time at job sites or driving between them. The work sample image links to a gallery of several dozen other examples of the company's work. A text link printed over the photo makes the gallery hard to miss. The site also features an attractive and, more important, unobtrusive background photo—a faded picture of a brick patio—a design detail that I think says a lot about the company's interest in aesthetics and doing quality work.

What I Would Change: The business might benefit from adding more information about itself on its home page, such as how long it has been in business, the names of its biggest customers, or even its physical address. The small type at the bottom of the page in part reads "We serve all Florida and Georgia"—that's something that should be larger and higher up on the page. Traffic counters are popular with small site owners because they offer a foolproof way to tally visits to a site, but most reputable hosting companies will provide site statistics that make these counters unnecessary. On this site, the page counter (lower-right corner) is more prominent than other critical information, such as the company phone number and free-estimate offer.

Summary

In this chapter, you learned some of the ways a small site for a trade-services company can benefit the business by answering basic questions, demonstrating dependability, setting it apart from the competition, and encouraging a response from visitors.

SMALL SITES FOR SPECIALTY PRODUCTS

13

- Learn how to create a small site for marketing a specialty product.

E very year, thousands of new products show up on supermarket shelves, department stores aisles, and cable TV infomercials, filling niche markets ranging from gourmet foods to cosmetic dentistry. As our society ages, brand loyalty grows stronger and new products are met with increasing skepticism.

Often, when presented with a new product, people think, "Why have you decided to make and sell another brand of widgets when there are already several dozen good brands on the market and I know which one I like?"

Your mousetrap may be better than everything that's come before it, but fewer and fewer people are willing to beat a path to your door to find out why.

Answering the Call

Your website's mission: To change that attitude by showing visitors that your product is worth the risk and that they won't regret changing their buying habits. Your small site should convince visitors to buy your product and give it a try—and it should enable them to tell friends about it if they're satisfied. A key to accomplishing this is a site that tells your unique story and makes a personal connection with your potential customers.

Advertisers have long used the technique of creating a problem the target market didn't know it had in order to sell the solution. A small site for a specialty product—especially an offbeat one—might benefit from a similar strategy. Also, don't discount the power of the Web in connecting your business with potential customers who seek out novel or unique products in order to maintain their status as trendsetters, first adopters, or someone "in the know."

A specialty product site is also likely to generate return visits from loyal customers who keep your web address among their bookmarked favorites. Planning for easy ways to keep your site's content fresh will reward customers who already love your product and will enhance the sense among new visitors that your wares are the product of fresh thinking.

Home-Page Helper

A picture of your product should be one of, if not *the,* dominant element of your home page. People need to know what it looks like before they buy it (see Figure 13.1).

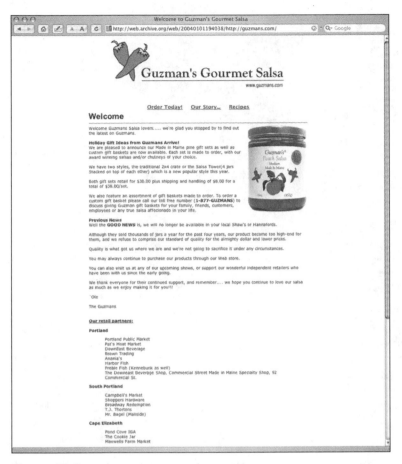

Figure 13.1
A site for a brand of gourmet salsa combines two key elements for product-oriented websites: a prominent photo of the product itself and a list of retail locations where it is sold.

If your product performs a function, you'll want to show it in action. If you're building small, you probably don't have the budget for a Flash-based presentation, but good news—you don't need one. You can get 90 percent of the effect of a Flash product demo with much less effort by using an animated GIF of your product in action. Even a gallery of still pictures showing your product in its various steps or configurations can be an effective demonstration of your product's capabilities, size, novel design, or other unique attributes (see Figure 13.2).

You also want your site to demonstrate your product's value by using customer testimonials or reviews to overcome the doubts—or indifference—of potential customers. If people really love your product, then you probably aren't wanting for positive comments and reviews. The trick when building small is to not get carried away with your own

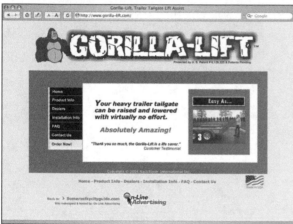

Figure 13.2
On the home page for Gorilla-Lift, a simple four-frame animated GIF demonstrates the product's ease of use—an attribute that this well-done small site shares.

good press and customer feedback. Try to limit the number of customer testimonials or review excerpts offered on your site to about half a dozen.

A where-to-buy page—a must-have for any product sold through retail channels—also can corroborate a product's legitimacy while giving new and repeat customers a useful resource. Pay attention to sales and specials on your product around town or on the Web and put that information on your site with your "where to buy" list (review the site shown in Figure 13.1). Tracking bargains, sales, coupons, and specials is a good way to introduce new people to your product and give sales an occasional boost. If you run pricing promotions, get the word out through sites like these.

SITE WALK-THROUGH: PORTABLEBOATS.COM

In this walk-through, we'll look at a purveyor of portable fishing boats (see Figure 13.3).

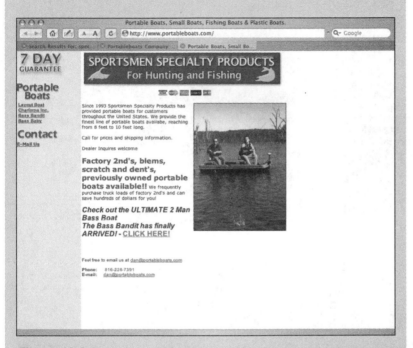

Figure 13.3
This site does a good job of showing off its specialty product: portable boats.

What I Like: Whether a website is designed to make a sale or just build interest, pictures of the featured products in use are a key to the site's success. This site offers a lot of photos—on the home page and on product pages—that show how, despite their portability, the boats can accommodate two full-grown men. The left side of the page clearly lists the four models available, the company's guarantee, and an email address to use to get more information.

What I Would Change: This site could benefit from a cleaner and more consistent use of color and a better connection between the website address (portableboats.com) and the company logo at the top of the page. Headings, like the ones in purple and blue, should be the same color and style, include action-oriented words, and be short enough to fit on one or two lines. Also, I think the logo looks too much like an advertisement for an unrelated company, which might confuse first-time visitors.

SITE WALK-THROUGH: SENTRYTABLEPAD.COM

In this walk-through, we'll look at the small site for a table pad manufacturer (see Figure 13.4).

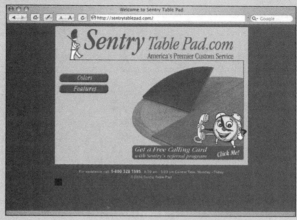

Figure 13.4
This site illustrates that the company can effectively market a specialty product like table pads using a small number of web pages.

What I Like: This simple four-page site packs a lot of useful information for potential customers. Like many sites, this site's home page (Figure 13.4, top) and subpages (Figure 13.4, bottom) share a common motif but not a common format. The distinction is handled well, with the home page serving as a greeter, the subpages presenting detailed and well-formatted product information, and all pages sharing elements like logo placement and navigation style. I even like the "Click Me" cartoon clock that calls attention to a free offer. Similar images like this are available on clip art sites all over the Web, but they are rarely used so well. At the bottom of the page, the call to action is a toll-free number listed conveniently alongside the company's business hours.

What I Would Change: The home page features what I think is a cryptic tagline—"America's Premier Custom Service"—while the hidden meta tag description reads, in part: "...supplying the Furniture Industry with table pads since 1911...servicing 5,000 dealers nationwide." That kind of short descriptive information would be an effective addition to the home page. Five thousand dealers is too many to list on a small site, but a "Where to Buy" page could list the names of major retail chains and an invitation to call the company for a list of dealers in a given area. Adding a new page of product care tips would be a good way to build customer loyalty and increase return visits. Finally, the ".com" in the home page header graphic is most likely a relic of the boom years—when companies of all shapes and sizes sought to append cyberspace awareness to their brand—and I would let it go.

Killer App

Using email to start and maintain a dialog between you and your customers will be the most valuable marketing tool on your small site.

If visitors to your website are interested in your story, they will want to come back for updates or will be willing to let you tell them the latest news. Start collecting email addresses from day one, even if you have no idea how to use them.

Since all you really need to collect are email addresses, you don't need a sophisticated form or mailing list application to get started. A "mailto" link can be enough to start pulling in a few addresses. Direct the message to a special address at your site—list@yourproduct.com—with a pre-filled subject line, such as "Email list request."

Offer an incentive for signing up, such as a Web-only coupon. If you're using the simple email link method, set up an auto-responder with your hosting company or ISP to reply to new sign-ups with a link to your weekly coupon. A more sophisticated mailing list system might reward joiners with a coupon that loads on the thank-you page following a successful form submission.

SITE WALK-THROUGH: HUGOANYWHERE.COM

In this walk-through, we'll review a site for the HUGO, a rolling walker with a seat (see Figure 13.5).

Figure 13.5
Specialty products come in all shapes and sizes, as do the sites that promote and sell them.

What I Like: The color scheme, rounded images, and smiling faces contribute to this site's appealing design. The images of the product in use clearly indicate its versatility and typical users. The navigation labels are well worded and positioned consistently at the top of the page throughout the site. A JavaScript dynamic HTML effect changes the primary navigation labels from yellow to white when the visitor passes their mouse pointer over them.

What I Would Change: The images on this site might be too much of a good thing, since the combined file size of the HTML code and all the images is more than 170 kilobytes. That's a lot to download for a target audience that is more likely to be using a dial-up modem than a high-speed connection. I would spend time optimizing images and removing some that are redundant. For example, the logo does not need to appear on the home page in two places, as it does now. The images also could benefit from the addition of alt tags, which present a text-based description of the image while it loads and, when worded correctly, can improve a site's search engine placement. Alt tags also allow visually impaired visitors a way to read and interact with a site through special screen-reader software.

The Word Is Out

Now, turn the email functionality around and let your repeat visitors do some marketing for you. Give your Web audience permission to forward your deals page or coupon page to others with a "tell a friend" link. As with the simple email link that you can use to collect addresses for your mailing list, you can set up an email link that puts the address for any page on your site in the body of an email with the address line blank.

Also keep in mind that your website has to be ready when your marketing efforts start to bear fruit. Word-of-mouth referrals may reach the so-called "tipping point" or your product and website address may get a coveted mention on a popular TV show. Be prepared for a spike in traffic. That's why it's so important (as I explained in Chapter 8) to run your site at a reputable hosting company. Program the tech support phone number in your cell phone when you set up the account. When you need the extra web server capacity, the hosting company will have it ready for you.

Keep It Small

Much of a specialty product's strength and growth potential lies in its uniqueness, so resist the urge to overbuild your site to the point that its indistinguishable from other bloated sites on the Web.

The Specialty Product Small Site Design Checklist

Here's a handy checklist to use to help you design your own specialty products small site.

- Your primary goal is to get potential customers to understand the unique value and quality of your product, ask for it by name, and purchase it.

- Show pictures of your products or product action shots where applicable.

- If you don't sell direct to the public on your site, make sure you include a where to buy or how to buy page or section.

- Clearly list the potential uses or varieties for the product you're trying to sell.

- Include information about your guarantee, warranty, or return policy.

- People will come to your site looking for all the information they can get about your product, but don't let too much information presented in one place keep you from closing the deal. Consider

Figure 13.6
Logos can provide visual cues about retail outlets for a product and publicity it has received.

offering product specifications or data sheets in PDF format that the user can download.

- Clearly display any awards, recognitions or notable publicity your product has received. Use visual cues where possible, like star ratings, "Best in Show" logos, or "As seen on…" endorsements (see Figure 13.6).

- Let your home page reflect the uniqueness of your product, but don't forget to keep it simple. Many of your potential customers have heard about you by word of mouth or an advertisement, so they aren't necessarily comparing your site to a lot of others like it.

- If you're doing other types of marketing, such as TV advertising or direct mail, you're best off working with a designer who can maintain visual consistency in your website and other media.

Summary

In this chapter, you learned some ways to extend a specialty product's marketing efforts with a small website. Sites for specialty products don't so much compete with other sites as they do with a visitor's decision to buy or not to buy. Use a small site to offer compelling information and images about a product's advantages and provide a clear pathway to encourage a customer to make a purchase.

SMALL SITES FOR ARTISTS, WRITERS, AND PERFORMERS

14

- Learn how to create a small site for a creative professional such as an artist, writer, or performer.

The so-called "creative class"—a growing segment of the U.S. workforce—includes people whose talents range from acting and animating to writing and web design. Even as they exhibit their talents through a variety of artistic outlets, creative types all have a common need for a website that contributes to the success of their business. A successful small site for a photographer, musician, or sculptor must offer both a unique expression of the artist's style *and* practical content and functionality for potential customers, patrons, and fans.

Answering the Call

Selling a creative talent is a lot like selling a specialty product (which I covered in Chapter 13). In the case of an artist's website, though, the product is the artist—that is, you. The "brand of you" is something that's on the mind of more and more people these days, and a website can be a powerful partner in establishing and maintaining your "brand." Before your visitors get to your portfolio or appearance schedule, your site has to give them an impression about the nature of your art, who you are, and what you have to offer.

Your website's design, of course, plays the leading role in defining you and your work for visitors. In fact, the best small sites for artists are online extensions of their work . You can easily extend your style and your brand onto your website by using your handwritten script or signature as part of your logo and navigation. See two good examples in Figures 14.1 and 14.2.

Home-Page Helper

There are many sites on the Web these days that are works of art in and of themselves. A small site for an artist's business should not be one of them. Instead, an artist's site has to confirm that the artistic pursuits described on the site are, in fact, a business. Doing so requires a more conventional (read non-artistic) approach to answering the basic who, what, and how of your business as well as specialized questions that visitors may be wondering, such as, "Do you work on commission?" or "Are you available for weddings?"

If it's nothing else, an artist's website should be an online flip book or sampler of the artist's work. Make it easy for people to see what the work looks like, either with a prominent link labeled "Gallery" or "Portfolio" or with actual work samples displayed on your home page

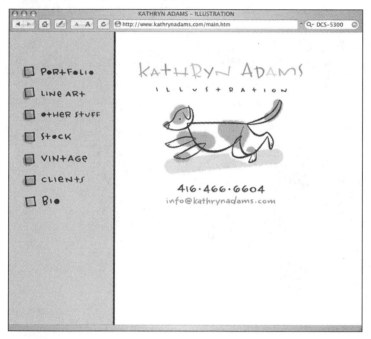

Figure 14.1
Kathryn Adams is not a dog trainer or veterinarian. She's an illustrator—a fact that's readily apparent within the first five seconds of visiting her site.

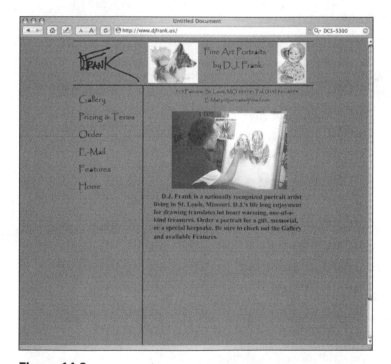

Figure 14.2
A St. Louis portrait artist wisely uses his own signature for his site logo and handwritten script for the navigation to give visitors and immediate impression of his work.

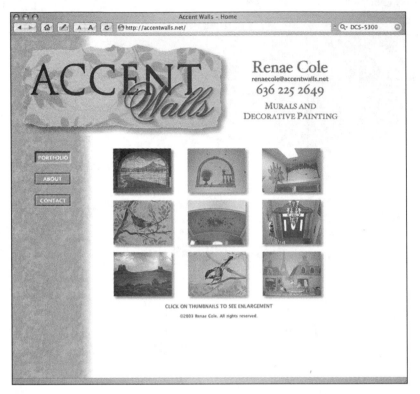

Figure 14.3
This artist's home page *is* her portfolio, which makes it easy to find on her site. The red text below the thumbnails reinforces the idea that clicking them will load a larger view.

(see Figure 14.3). Give visitors a chance to get a good look at your work by linking thumbnails to larger versions, or use a web authoring program like Dreamweaver to create a slide show of samples. Remember to size your largest images so they fit within the confines of a typical browser window—about 800x600 pixels.

You can also strengthen the case for your business with a list of high-profile clients or customer testimonials. If you've done work for some well-known clients, list them by name or logo on your home page. Collect a few choice quotes from satisfied customers and compile the best ones on a testimonials page.

Site updates are another way to express the business side of your artistic talents. Set aside a corner of your home page to list news about upcoming and ongoing exhibitions, performances, or appearances. But resist your artistic urge to design a unique page every time you have something new to post on your site. Keep your site updates simple and consistent.

SITE WALK-THROUGH: GEORGEWEBBER.COM

In this walk-through, we'll look at the small site for California historian and actor George Webber (see Figure 14.4).

Figure 14.4
A California-based actor provides a good model for a creative small site.

What I Like: The home page for georgewebber.com uses photos, text, and dynamic mouse rollover effects to clearly exhibit the versatile talents of the site's subject. Instead of conjuring up some kind of artificial and potentially confusing navigation scheme, the creator of this site organized it around George Webber's personas. The subpages are self-contained portrayals of his various performances, including additional photos, testimonials, and offers for promotional videos where available. The site also uses a clever contact device. Instead of using a consistent "Contact Me" or "Contact George Webber" link, each page includes a link to contact the character described on that page. Creating unique email addresses for each character is a simple and effective way to extend his performances into the online world. They also allow him to track online interest in his various offerings and respond with unique "in-character" answers for each message sent via his website.

What I Would Change: There's not much to change on this small site. I often recommend that small personal sites for artists—like this one—present the subject's name as the largest graphical element on the site. But this site's focus on learning about the characters rather the man behind them could suffer by following that advice. Where the site does suffer is in its use of microcontent (covered in detail in

Chapter 5). Things like a page title tagline, meta tag keywords and descriptions, and alt tag image descriptions—largely missing from this site—are an easy and inexpensive way to improve search-engine placement and click-through.

Killer App

Throughout this book I have argued against the use of website gimmicks. The site add-ons and doodads that are supposed to make a site hip or edgy just end up making it larger and cluttered. But often an artist's job is to challenge the status quo. And, as is true in other areas of society, I think artists can get away with more "rule bending" on their websites than other business owners can. On their sites, artists should be free to experiment with animations, sounds, nonstandard page designs, and other web tricks in the name of artistic expression— provided they pertain to the work of the website's subject (see Figure 14.5). But going overboard with avant-garde design tricks on an artist's site will lead to the same result doing so on a non-artistic site will lead to visitors giving up on your site and leaving in frustration.

Figure 14.5
Here's a website you have to *hear* to believe. The sample loop of the subject's music that plays automatically when the home page loads is a good example of an appropriate use of a website add-on that would be hard to justify on a different kind of website.

SITE WALK-THROUGH: MIRACLESTUDIOS.COM

This walk-through covers the site for a high-end animation studio (see Figure 14.6).

Figure 14.6
Here's a small site created by a slightly larger firm that specializes in creating custom illustrations and animations.

What I Like: For a company that does illustration and animation work for both IBM and Ozzy Osbourne, the design of this site is refreshingly restrained. Perhaps the owners are like a cobbler too busy to fix the holes in his own shoes. Or perhaps they know that that a simple site like this one is all they need to get the job done. Three main navigation buttons—Contact, Portfolio, and About—cover the majority of questions that visitors and potential customers will have when they visit the site: Who are you and what do you do? What does your work look like? How can I get in touch with you to hire you or find out more?

What I Would Change: A company like this one surely uses Flash in its everyday work, so the use of Flash on its website—for the home page animation, among other things—is not a surprise. (I would be more surprised if the site featured no Flash at all.) The site builders wisely let the Flash-animated logo on the home page share screen space with meaningful information rather than placing it alone on what would be an ambiguous and frivolous splash page. But even Flash usage that complements a site—as it does here—can have its drawbacks. The home page animation weighs in at a more than 900 kilobytes, and the Portfolio page features a whopping 2.3-megabyte Flash component. Lest you turn away potential customers on a slow or sluggish Internet connection, it's better to optimize animations like these to the smallest acceptable file size and give a clear indication that a page may take a while to load.

SITE WALK-THROUGH: CLAIREPHOTOGRAPHY.COM

For this walk-through, let's look at the small site for a St. Louis photographer (see Figure 14.7).

Figure 14.7
With this small site, a St. Louis photographer really puts her talents to work in showing off her art form.

What I Like: A nice combination of color and composition is used on this site to present a usable online gallery of the photographer's work. Her black-and-white self-portrait says a lot about her sense of style and technique, while the full-color gallery samples at the bottom of the home page really stand out on a base of black, white, and red. The subpages are arranged as thumbnail grids that link into slide show details for each of the three work areas featured on the site. The easy-to-find phone number at the top of the page gives visitors a clear cue about what they need to do to find out more.

What I Would Change: The dense block of small type on the home page seems out of place on a site that is otherwise a well-metered overview of the photographer's work. The text could be reformatted for better readability by increasing the font size, adding space between lines and to the right and left margins, or summarizing it into a series of bullet points and shorter paragraphs. The site's usability falters a bit on some of the Information pages, where links to subpages open in new browser windows. Sites that spawn extra windows can easily confuse visitors or lead them to doubt a site's integrity.

The Word Is Out

Getting new visitors to come to an artist's website requires creative thinking. Fortunately, many people in a creative line of work have regular access to large groups of potential visitors to their website. These groups are also called "the audience." Whether its through stage performances, exhibitions of your work, or some other venue, offline-to-online marketing strategies (explained in more detail in Chapter 6) offer the best opportunities for attracting new visitors to your site and building up a group of repeat visitors.

When you know your work will have an audience, make sure your website address gets part of the spotlight, too. At coffeehouse displays of their paintings, artists should make sure their calling card includes not only the title of the piece and its price, but an online address as well. Musicians who send out demos should print their URL on the CD. Actors, don't be frightened to request second billing for your website address in bios printed in stage bills and other promotional materials.

The Artist Small Site Design Checklist

Here's a handy checklist to use to help you design your own artist's small site.

- Your primary goal regarding visitors to your site is to make an impression about the creative talents you offer.

- State your areas of specialization clearly, concisely, and accurately. Don't fall into the trap of trying to be too general.

- Provide a list of clients or credentials, be they publications in which your work has appeared or performing workshops at which you've participated.

- If you work with a network of other artists who provide services related to yours, provide information about it. You might want to include a "related services" page. This will help show a potential customer that you are part of an established community of creative professionals.

- If you have received awards or favorable press, provide that information or links to the appropriate sites or publications.

- Try to keep your home page really simple. Remember that potential customers who come to your site are likely searching for a particular kind of artist and that they've probably seen other sites before they get to yours.

- Spend some time looking at other sites that provide services similar to yours.

- Avoid complicated navigation features. This is not where you want to show off the latest website design techniques.

- If you have the skills to design your own site, you'll benefit from being able to make it an online expression of your artistic talents.

- If you employ the services of a web designer to create a site for you, make sure the designer has experience in creating the type of site that you need. Don't let the designer get carried away in adding features you really don't need.

Summary

In this chapter, you learned that creators of artists' sites can exercise more freedom in website design and functionality than they can with other types of sites. However, success can be expected only with sites that balance such unique artistic expressions with nuts-and-bolts answers to visitors' questions.

SMALL SITES FOR RESTAURANTS
15

- Learn how to create a small site for a restaurant or entertainment business.

U nlike a site for a doctor—where a successful visit may lead to an office visit several days later—or a specialty products site—where fulfillment might come four to six weeks hence—visitors to restaurant websites arrive seeking immediate gratification. Many may show up at your establishment within hours of using your website. They are hungry—for information about your business, and maybe a good meal, too. A successful restaurant website will give its visitors the same level of service they'll get in person, and it won't keep them waiting to get it. When they're done, they'll leave the site feeling satisfied.

Answering the Call

The website for a restaurant—or any kind of related establishment, such as bars and nightclubs—must give visitors an online experience that prepares them for the real-world experience. With so many restaurants to choose from, only a website that helps people picture themselves dining at your establishment can be considered a success.

Your site has to convey what, if anything, is distinctive about your place in terms of the visitor's immediate needs: Is this place close to my house? Does it serve the kind of food I want? Should I make a reservation? What kind of amenities and ambience does it offer? Will there be live music tonight? Has this place been well reviewed—or reviewed at all?

The last thing you want to do is surprise people by giving one impression about your establishment on your website and another when they're actually there. People eating out don't like a surprise (unless it's their birthday), and those that get one are unlikely to come back to your restaurant *or* your website.

Home-Page Helper

Like any site that is designed to attract online visitors to a physical location, a restaurant website can benefit from providing visual cues. On your home page, try to include a street-level picture of your location or an interior picture of your dining room. If at all possible, make sure some of your tables are occupied with people (see Figure 15.1).

I don't think many visitors to a restaurant website spend a lot of time reading wordy home pages, so don't feel compelled to write something new in order to fill the space. Concentrate on making sure there are quick and clear links and bite-size morsels of information that give

Figure 15.1
The exterior and dining room shots on this Alexandria,
Virginia, restaurant's website help potential diners know what
to expect. I just wish they were in color.

people a taste of your restaurant before they get there. Include your logo
and a description of the cuisine you serve and consider these must-have
navigation choices: Menu, Map, Reservations, and Reviews. If you offer
services for large groups and special events, think about adding these
navigation choices as necessary: Catering, Facilities, and Calendar.

Killer App

While artists and musicians can provide visual and audio samples of
their work over the Web, it may be a while before websites that can offer
smells and tastes become commonplace (see Figure 15.2). Nonetheless,
there are a handful of functionality options for a restaurant website that
will gratify visitors without overwhelming your ability to keep up.

If you're committed to making more of your site than the average restaurant owner would, look to a site such as marcoscafe.com (see Figure
15.3) for inspiration. The daily specials and soup du jour (icons in the
upper-left corner of the home page) are kept fresh daily. Having features
like this helps keep the site interesting, but they do take time to support.

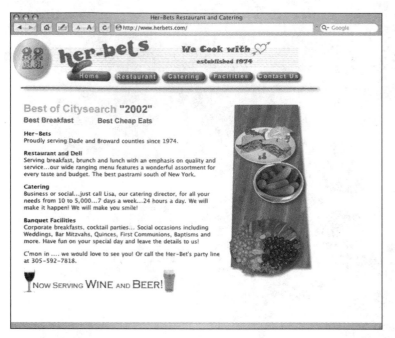

Figure 15.2
For your eyes only: Menu samples on a Miami restaurant's home page look good enough to eat, but actually doing so requires time away from the computer.

Figure 15.3
The marcoscafe.com site makes me hungry for the daily specials. Having a feature like this can help persuade a customer to book a reservation for the evening.

One of the easiest ways to extend your site's usefulness is to offer your menu as both a web page and a download. Your patrons will want to keep one handy for choosing an out-to-dinner spot for out-of-town guests or simply to place a take-out order. Next time you revise your menu, have your designer export the layout as a PDF file, which can be viewed with Adobe software installed on just about every computer these days. You might also consider keeping a plain-text version of your current menu handy for use by restaurant guide sites such as Citysearch.

Many restaurants also are starting to experiment with online reservations, either through third-party systems such as OpenTable.com or using home-grown methods where email replaces the tried-and-true telephone. Be careful not to fall for high-tech temptations in the hope that it alone can make your website better. When you opt for using advanced functionality like this, make sure it offers a better alternative than traditional methods and you have the staff training and workflow in place to handle the change.

SITE WALK-THROUGH: WWW.HURLEYS-RESTAURANT.COM

In this walk-through, we'll examine a site for an upscale restaurant in Portland, Oregon (see Figure 15.4).

What I Like: Even though the home page doesn't feature a lot of copy, it tells me a lot about the place. Three clearly worded and arranged navigation choices—Reservations, Winelist, and Reviews—suggest that Hurley's is an upscale establishment where I might enjoy a gourmet meal. The photo of the dining room conveys a lot about the ambience diners enjoy at the restaurant (even though the tables have no diners sitting at them). The bottom of every page on the site also shows a modification date, which, thanks to a small and easy-to-implement piece of HTML code, can do a lot to bolster how visitors perceive the dependability of the business behind the site. The pages on this site all showed a recent date when I visited, so I know someone has been working on the site fairly recently.

What I Would Change: I like the layout of this home page so much—the way the photos overlap into an appealing montage—that it almost makes me want to forget that the site could benefit from having a bit more information on its opening page. For example, what kind of food is served here? What are the business hours? How often does the menu change? I'd also recommend that the contact information in the upper-right corner be redone as text created as HTML rather than a graphic that can't be copied and pasted into an email or address book.

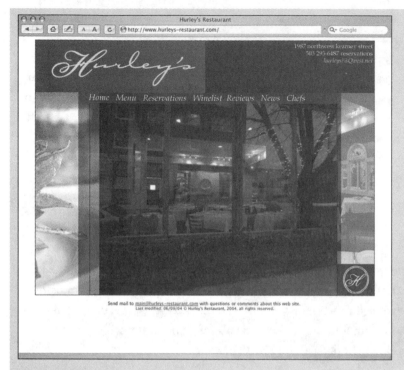

Figure 15.4
The owners of Hurley's do a good job of using a website to position their restaurant for upscale clientele.

SITE WALK-THROUGH: WWW.THECARLIN.COM

Let's now take a look at a Billings, Montana, nightclub in this walk-through (see Figure 15.5) to see how the owners of a different type of establishment market their offerings.

What I Like: The home page shown is actually about two and half screen's worth of scrolling on a typical monitor. The top third of the main page offers just about everything I want to know about a nightclub in a small, sophisticated package. There are easy-to-spot red buttons that link to the club's schedule of events and appetizer menu. The logo at the top center of the page matches the sign shown in the picture of the building on the left side of the page, so I know what to look for if I'm going for the first time. An easy-to-read box on the right side outlines the regular drink specials and events that the club offers. For all the images and text presented on this page, the owners have done visitors on slow web connections a favor by optimizing everything down to about 60 kilobytes.

What I Would Change: The page seems to have a split personality, with each one geared toward a different audience. There's certainly nothing wrong with an establishment offering targeted promotions for its varied clientele, but I

Figure 15.5
This establishment has a number of entertainment offerings and its site provides a good showcase for what is available.

think the artists' bios and other marketing copy filling up the bottom two-thirds of the home page should be given their own subpages or left off the site altogether. Most visitors will only want to know who's playing, when, and how much it costs, and the Schedule of Events page offers most of that information. A simple change could make that information available on the home page, too. I also would redo the update text in the upper right corner from a graphic to plain text coded into the HTML tags on the page. Doing so would make the text both easier to update for someone without access or experience using image-editor software *and* accessible to search-engine indexing. Using text instead of a graphic also enables visitors to easily copy and paste it into an email for friends. Finally, the contact information at the bottom of the page doesn't include an area code with the phone number. I know Montana is a big place with an area code all to itself, but out-of-towners looking for a place to go for happy hour might not know what it is.

A Lawrence, Kansas, restaurant gets a once-over in this walk-through (see Figure 15.6).

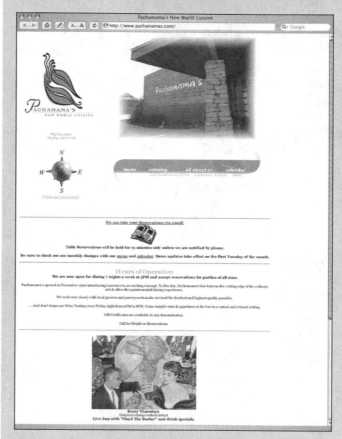

Figure 15.6
This restaurant site provides a good model for how the important but basic information for a restaurant can be communicated.

What I Like: The content of the home page covers most of the basics that people want to know about a restaurant: address and phone number, a link to a map, an exterior photograph, the hours of operation, a brief description, and an offer to take a reservation by email. The green color scheme of the navigation buttons effectively reinforces the "New World Cuisine" tagline, which I interpret to mean a simple, earthy, and natural dining experience. The interior photos used on subpages bear this out, showing an establishment with lots of natural light, limestone brick walls, and light-colored wood trim.

What I Would Change: The logo on the website does not match the logo shown on the side of the building in the home page image. I'm probably the only one who notices things like this, but I think the discrepancy could create a sub-conscious impression in a visitor's mind that perhaps this place hasn't quite established itself yet. The site's navigation should be moved to the top of the page, above the photo and closer to the logo. The compass rose (an animated GIF when viewed in a browser) that calls attention to the map page needs to be moved away from the logo to keep them from competing with each other, or just dropped altogether. A "Location" link in the main navigation would be a better place to link to the map page. The text on the home page, while brief and infor-mative, needs some help. The address (under the navigation) and phone number (under the logo) need to be in a larger, darker typeface to improve readability. Reformatting the main text of the page into shorter, left-justified lines in a larger serif typeface will improve its readability, too.

The Restaurant Small Site Checklist

Here's a handy checklist to use to help you design your own restaurant's small site.

- Your primary goal is to turn site visitors into patrons of your estab-lishment. On your home page, make sure you put your address and, especially if you take reservations or call-in orders, your phone number.

- Clearly state what and when you serve with information about hours of operation and links to your menu or menus.

- If you offer package deals with nearby hotels, theaters, bars, or other businesses, make sure you provide this information. Link to your partners' businesses and get them to link to your site.

- Offer a PDF download of your menu or a coupon for website visitors.

- Clearly display any awards, recognitions, or notable publicity your establishment has received. Use visual cues where possible, like star ratings or "Best of..." logos.

- If you don't have reviews, provide a list of customer testimonials.

- Let your home page reflect the uniqueness of your establishment, but don't forget to keep it simple. Many of your potential patrons have heard about you by word of mouth or an advertisement, so they aren't necessarily comparing your site to a lot of others like it.

- Even if your visitors don't, you should spend some time looking at sites of businesses that are competitive with yours.

- Avoid complicated navigation features. This is not where you want to show off the latest website design techniques.

- If you employ the services of a web designer to create a site for you, make sure that the designer has experience in creating the type of site you need. Don't let the designer get carried away in adding features you really don't need.

Summary

Web surfers are an impatient breed, and never more so than at feeding time. To be successful online, a restaurant must provide a website that feeds visitors' appetite for information about the dining experience.

INDEX

W